JUMP FOR IT!

"This is a real thriller of the air."—*Star*

"In each of these incidents the description of courage beyond belief is cripplingly vivid. In each of them one's already unbounded admiration for the RAF is urged to even greater intensity."—*Sunday Times*

JUMP FOR IT!

Stories of the Caterpillar Club

GERALD BOWMAN

UNABRIDGED

PAN BOOKS LTD : LONDON

First published 1955 by Evans Bros. Ltd.
This edition published 1957 by Pan Books Ltd.,
8 Headfort Place, London, S.W.1

Printed in Great Britain by Richard Clay and Company, Ltd.,
Bungay, Suffolk

CONTENTS

ILLUSTRATIONS

IN PHOTOGRAVURE

(*between pages 96 and 97*)

For permission to reproduce the photographs in this book, the publishers are indebted to: The Air Ministry; Charles E. Brown; Central Press; Fox Photos; Imperial War Museum; *Picture Post*; Topical Press.

FOREWORD

If you are looking for the sort of heroics which turn RAF personnel pink with embarrassment—or render them helpless with laughter—you will not find such matter in these pages. All I have done here is to set down the personal stories of men who have saved their own lives by taking to their parachutes.

Men who have been forced to do this automatically become members of the 'Caterpillar Club', which was founded by Leslie Irvin, the designer (and original demonstrator) of the world's first successful free-type parachute.

At the time of writing there are well over 40,000 members, by far the greater number of whom 'joined' during the Second World War. (If you ask one of them about the 'Club', he usually answers: 'There's no formality—we're not exclusive—anyone can join who just likes to drop in.') The caterpillar, of course, symbolizes the silk from which the original parachute canopies were woven. Nowadays the fabric is nylon.

Each of these stories was told me by the man concerned, or has been taken from official records. Each man has been given the opportunity to read what I have written and make his own cuts or alterations. In taking this course my main object has been to ensure that I did not unwittingly over-dramatise any incident, or put anyone in the position of having 'shot an appalling line'.

The first story, that concerning ex-P/O W. B. Parker, is, I will admit, placed out of context. I decided to give it pride of place, however, since it is the most astounding record of human fortitude in my experience, and will give the reader a clear idea of what he may expect to find within these covers.

Gerald Bowman

1

CANOPY OF FIRE

On October 8th, 1940, Pilot Officer W. B. Parker, a twenty-five-year-old officer of the Royal New Zealand Air Force, made what is probably the most terrifying parachute descent in the history of war—that is, if one excepts those fortunately rare incidents in which the parachute failed to open.

Parker was at that time one of the band of pioneer pilots who started flying over enemy territory and photographing German naval bases, ports, airfields and cities. At the outbreak of war it had been intended that this work should be done by Blenheim aircraft, but the unsung heroes who made the attempt soon found that their planes were no match for the German fighters, and they were often unable to get to the objectives marked down. The number of photographs obtained had to be accounted for against the heavy number of pilots who were never heard of again, or who finished up in German prison camps. Something, therefore, had to be done about it.

F. S. Cotton, a civilian air-survey operator working with the late Flight Lieutenant M. V. Longbottom, suggested that a really fast, high-flying aircraft like a Spitfire should be fitted with cameras, but with no guns. Without the weight of armament the Spitfire would be able to outclimb any enemy, and would be faster and quicker in manœuvre. Moreover, if the Spitfire were fitted with long-range tanks which could be dropped, it would be able to penetrate deep into enemy territory, and it would still be in a position to lighten itself and run if it met unexpected attack.

As all Service people know now, this idea proved tremendously successful from the time it was first tried out by the courageous pioneers. It took courage to fly a totally unarmed aircraft deep into enemy territory, an operation which often included long and lonely crossings of hundreds of miles of ocean in any kind of weather. Later on in the war this special kind of work became the task of the famous PRU (Photographic Reconnaissance Unit), the members of which were said to be the first to encounter gremlins.

Meanwhile, Parker and his companions had come to a base at Heston aerodrome and at St Eval in Cornwall, to which they had returned after earlier operations in France, before the evacuation.

By October 1940 Parker had completed twenty-six operational flights with the unit. He had already brought back a mass of valuable photographs of enemy territory and shipping dispositions in the Channel ports. During a routine flight from Cap Gris Nez to the Scheldt in the previous month he had spotted one of the first concentrations of barges and boats which the Germans were massing in preparation for the invasion. It was this, together with a mass of information, later brought back, which gave accurate targets for intensive bombing attacks and caused the Nazi High Command to think better of the whole idea.

October 8th was a bright, clear morning of autumn with the sun warm and benign against a vast curtain of clear blue, and forming a death-trap for any airman without his eyes peeled. Parker knew its dangers well enough as he warmed up his engine, waved the chocks away, and then thundered off down the runway to do his job of photographing various Dutch and French ports. At that moment the sun-glare, and the enemy aircraft it might hide, did not worry him overmuch. He intended to put a good 30000 feet beneath him before he set out to cross the Channel. Then, as he took his photographs through the telescopic lens of the camera, he would be far above the hornet's nest of enemy Messerschmitts and able to get well away in his unarmed aircraft if he saw any of them coming up for him. He would also be high enough to be reasonably safe from getting 'jumped' out of the sun-glare, since no heavily-armed aircraft could hang about cruising at that altitude.

From Heston he climbed steadily, watching his altimeter, until, when he was somewhere over the middle of Kent, he saw it registering 29000 feet. Throughout the long climb his attention had automatically been on the sun side of the aircraft, but at this height he wasn't anticipating trouble.

Therefore, trouble chose just that moment to arrive, as is usual with airmen off guard.

Two Me109 fighter aircraft suddenly materialized out of the glare and attacked him from the rear. Parker did not catch sight of them. He had no idea that there was any other machine within five miles of him when a burst of cannon shell ripped past him into his engine, which jarred violently and then stopped dead. He saw fire blasting back between his knees and realized that there was nothing to do but get out. He slammed his canopy back and began knocking undone his radio leads and safety harness; the aircraft shuddered as a second burst of cannon shells went home.

This burst penetrated one of the petrol tanks, so that he was blinded and sprayed with the fuel as he finally managed to kick himself clear and go head-first over the side.

At 29000 feet a man cannot stay conscious for more than a minute or so without extra supplies of oxygen, and Parker knew it. He grabbed for the rip-cord of his parachute and jerked it almost as soon as he was clear of the blazing Spitfire. Then he passed out.

From that point until he reached around 10000 feet, swinging beneath his parachute he was unable to take any interest in the proceedings. When he regained consciousness he did it slowly and in the dazed, semi-detached manner peculiar to a victim of anoxia. He saw the vast green relief map of the earth swaying gently beneath him. He remembered the hectic moments of abandoning his aircraft and reflected that he was still alive, although of the shattered machine and his two enemies there was no sign.

Then, as his consciousness cleared, he smelled burning. He looked around and downwards, and realized for the first time that he himself was on fire. Already the petrol with which he had been sprayed had burned the lower part of his flying-suit. His hands were raw as he started frantically to beat out the flames. Petrol had soaked into the sponge rubber of his parachute cushion, which was well alight. He tore at it and wrenched away burning chunks of rubber; showers of sparks flew up, and his petrol-soaked flying-suit took fire around his face. He realized then that the whole of his equipment must have been soaked before he got out of the aircraft, because some of the rigging lines and part of his parachute canopy were alight in several places.

As a result, the speed of his descent increased and with the stronger draught the flames burned more fiercely.

It was at this point, when to observers below he looked more like a falling torch than a living man, that Parker gave up all hope. He decided that a quick death was much preferable to a slow one. He was in intense pain. The earth was still a long way below and his burning suit was flaming more briskly.

Parker reached for his chest, turned the quick-release gear of his parachute-harness, and banged it undone. In the next second he should have dropped clean away and fallen down the remaining thousands of feet to inevitable but mercifully-sudden death. As it was, only the two shoulder-straps of his harness jerked away and left him. In the next second he had pitched upside-down, feeling the thigh-straps of the harness slide down his legs and jam round his ankles.

There he hung helplessly while the flames of his burning flying-suit now played in the opposite direction. The fire travelled up his legs to his leather flying-boots and died away. Then one of the burning thigh-straps parted in a small shower of sparks, and Parker was left hanging by one foot.

By this time, owing to the severe burns on his face, he was temporarily blind. Although he was now very close to the earth he could not see it. Therefore, hanging upside-down at the moment of landing, he could make no effort to protect himself when he dropped heavily into the middle of a ploughed field.

The thudding force of the impact broke one of his arms in two places and almost knocked him out. Yet he was still conscious when those who had been watching his descent dashed to pick him up. At which point Pilot Officer Parker remarked cheerfully, if a little hoarsely, "Nice work, chaps—fielded on the first bounce!"

. . . . .

You will be pleased, if perhaps a little surprised, to hear that Mr W. B. Parker is today the perfectly healthy and happy father of a family in Blenheim, New Zealand, the town in which he was born on November 16th, 1914. He is, in fact, a public accountant, which means chartered accountant in England. He met his wife in Walton-on-Thames, three years after his appalling experience, and they now have a boy and two girls ranging in age from two to seven. And he still likes flying.

Parker is so typical of the best of the RAF, that after being patched up in Canterbury and other hospitals, he was, at his own request, posted back for flying duty with another photographic reconnaissance squadron. He flew a further tour of operations, being finally demobilized with the rank of Flight Lieutenant on August 22nd, 1945.

I have a letter from him lying in front of me. The first line is typical :

'For heaven's sake don't turn this into a line-shoot. If you have access to Air Ministry records, you'll find it in the papers of the old PDU [Photographic Development Unit, which was the predecessor of the Photographic Reconnaissance Unit], but please don't make it sound too hair-raising.'*

Here is another line from Parker's letter :

'As far as trying to drop out of the parachute is concerned, I suppose it must sound rather far-fetched, but by that time I was burning pretty freely and the position became somewhat hectic. I eventually decided that, rather than fight a slow death dangling on the end of a parachute, I would let go altogether and end it as quickly as possible. And I can assure you that if the same thing happened again my reactions would probably be the same. I cannot imagine any worse or more painful death than being burnt at the stake. Actually I was pretty lucky. Although I didn't realize it on the way down, I was being followed both by the Observer Corps and chaps from the Royal Army Medical Corps who, fortunately, were handy. This was because of the long trail of smoke I was leaving down the sky. Again, although I didn't know it until afterwards, the ploughed field in which I ended up was near the village of Wingham in Kent.'

Well, there it is. In these days, when high-powered psychiatrists get up in open court and excuse the most revolting forms of murder on the grounds that someone frightened the murderer in his youth with a golliwog, it

* I have checked all records of this in the first volume of the official *History of New Zealand in the Second World War* written by Wing Commander H. L. Thompson. I can promise you that the official report is rather more vivid than my own.

may be difficult to believe that a man like Parker can go through such an appalling experience, and survive to live a normal happy life as a respectable citizen with no damage to his nervous system. Since I am not a psychiatrist, but merely one who had the handling of over 3000 British, Commonwealth and American fighter pilots during the late war, I don't find such a thing very difficult to believe, after all.

Of men like Parker, rather than call them brave, I would say that they are unusually high examples of the normal. For I have found in my experience that normal, decent men can pull a very tough standard of bravery out of the bag when it comes to the pinch; and that, I am quite certain, is how they would rather be described.

Young Parker was keen on flying before the war broke out, and had his first air experience in the New Zealand Civil Reserve. Early in 1939, when war was obviously inevitable, he took a short course in the Royal New Zealand Air Force and then, after the start of hostilities, transferred on a short-service commission to the Royal Air Force, coming to England in 1940. The incident I have recorded was the only time that he had to bale out during the whole course of his operational flying.

A final line from his letter is informative.

> 'Somehow, I never had any premonition that I should have to bale out. Arguments often arose in the Mess as to whether one *would* bale out if the occasion arose. Personally, I always maintained that I would be prepared to do so, but a good many of my friends said they wouldn't under any circumstances. At least I proved my point. . . .'

He also proved a point which most airmen believe to be a fundamental truth. No man goes before his time.

2

CATERPILLAR MAN

THE world-famous 'Caterpillar Club' was founded by a young American, Leslie Irvin. He it was who invented the first really reliable 'free' parachute, which is attached only to the man who uses it and not in any way to the aircraft. This parachute was subsequently adopted by the Air Forces of Britain and America. Irvin conceived the idea thereafter of presenting every man whose life had been saved by an Irvin parachute with a tiny gold caterpillar, on the back of which was engraved the individual's name. The 'Club', therefore, has no imposing premises in the West End of London, or anywhere else. It exists only as a name—and as a highly efficient index-system of members' names kept at the British headquarters of the Irvin organization. Nevertheless it is, perhaps, the most exclusive club in the world.

Of Irvin's career, and his 300 jumps from aircraft while testing his own invention, I shall have more to say later. But here, for a little while, I think it would be interesting to take a quick look at the ideas men have had upon the subject and the attempts they made before the young Irvin came upon the scene.

Although the idea of mechanical flight was still laughed at by the general public until the turn of the last century, men of scientific mind had long realized the strong force that air has upon a falling object. The first primitive thinker undoubtedly realized it from the behaviour of falling leaves or feathers, and it was put to use before the dawn of written history in the form of sails, for, after all, any sailing vessel is only a form of parachute going in a horizontal direction. There are records going back many hundreds of years of men using sail-like canopies in an effort to break their fall when jumping from heights. However, it was not until the year 1802 that a really safe and scientifically designed parachute was made and tested by one Garnerim, a Frenchman. This was not a 'free' type. It was fastened to the aircraft (in this case a balloon) and not to the pilot, but in general shape and design it was amazingly like the parachutes of today. When inflated, it was an inverted cup shape, 23 feet in diameter and containing 870 square feet of material. But instead of hanging in a harness, Garnerim sat in a wicker basket which was attached beneath.

After four successful releases in France, Garnerim brought his contraption to England, where thousands of people, including the then Duke of York, Lord Stanhope and a number of Members of Parliament, assembled to watch him make his ascent by balloon from the Volunteer Ground in London. Garnerim had the whole contraption fixed to the balloon by a rope leading down to his basket, which he could cut through with a knife when he wanted to descend. The parachute hung beneath the balloon in folded form like a furled umbrella with the basket beneath. When the whole thing rose into the air 'it seemed that every heart beat in unison', according to an eye-witness account.

Since there was very little wind, the balloon travelled slowly across the country . . . 'in its majestic rise, passing through light and thin vapour and soon entering a very cold atmosphere which the brave aeronaut stated later indicated that he had gained a high altitude'.

This modest speed enabled the crowd to keep up, horsemen and men on foot running and galloping wildly across the wide fields and meadows on the fringe of the city, which are now solid masses of bricks and mortar. Then came the moment when Garnerim decided to come down. To let the following crowd know what he was about to do, he tossed a flag out of the basket as a prearranged signal. Then he drew his knife and 'with a hand firm from a conscience void of reproach, and which had never been lifted against anyone but in the field of victory', he slashed through the supporting cord . . . at a height he judged to be around 8000 feet.

According to the eye-witness the crowd yelled in horror as the two objects parted company with alarming suddenness, the balloon rising sharply and Garnerim in his basket falling like a stone directly beneath. But after only a short drop the parachute suddenly opened out like an umbrella, inflated fully, and could be seen firmly supporting the man in his basket whilst coming down the sky at a gentle speed. At which moment Garnerim stated later that, "I saw that my calculations were just, and my mind remained calm and serene".

Since his load, with ballast, was 230 pounds beneath a spread of 870 square feet, he was a good deal below the figure of safety for parachutes of today. At this rate his descent would be roughly what he estimated—about 10 feet per second. He would have done better to design for the modern rate of descent of 21 feet per second, which means less penduluming, and results in a final landing with the force of a jump off a 10-foot wall. There was also the question of ballast which he need not have carried at all and which didn't help matters.

As Garnerim came down the sky he began to pendulum violently, and found the swing was so wild that at one moment his basket was on a level with the canopy. This, of course, was partly caused by having no vent in the canopy top to allow the air to escape. He managed to correct the fault slightly by heaving out his ballast but, as he said afterwards, he realized that if he landed, "with the force of one of those prodigious swings, I might well kill myself as well as some of those who might be immediately beneath me".

The crowd, however, in the usual way of crowds, foresaw no danger to themselves but only to the brave man they were watching. They raced to a point directly underneath him as he came down, and fought amongst themselves to reach up and catch him as he dropped among them. Naturally, some of them were bowled over like ninepins, but the landing was safe and Garnerim stepped from his basket totally unhurt, but very green in the face, to be wildly embraced in a most un-English manner by those around.

In the first seconds after his arrival Garnerim tried to gather his parachute and fold it up, but the crowd would have none of it. They hoisted him up shoulder-high and carried him away in triumph. One of the Members of Parliament who had picked up the tricolour flag he had dropped before descending, marched ahead of the procession waving it triumphantly. What might have happened after that it is impossible to say, had not the Duke of York ordered a squadron of cavalry who were in attendance to ride through the crowd and rescue him. This was a timely act, for Garnerim's ride on the shoulders of the crowd 'occasioned him much discomfort, for the previous swinging in his parachute had upset his feelings, and before the procession had proceeded far he was obliged to ask them to desist, while he vomited'.

Even then his trials were not over, for, in the course of being rescued by the cavalry, he had one of his feet trodden on by a horse and somewhat damaged. However, great triumphs followed. His parachute was rescued and afterwards exhibited in Paris at the Pantheon, where thousands of people came to see it. And the balloon from which he had cut adrift was also rescued from where it had finally landed in Farnham, Surrey, 36 miles away.

From that day over a century passed before the vital need of a parachute that could save men from crashing or burning aircraft became apparent. At the end of that time all who were attempting to design safe parachutes followed Garnerim's original ideas. Meanwhile, a strange and tragic event was already in the making.

Amongst the crowd who watched Garnerim's thrilling

descent was an English lad named Robert Cocking. In a natural youthful way he immediately made Garnerim his personal hero, and for the next thirty years the idea of the parachute, and his own designs and models, took up all his spare time. Unfortunately, however, Cocking lacked a scientific mind, with the result that after trying a simple experiment, which he interpreted in entirely the wrong way, he brought about his own death. Cocking's experiment was simply that of dropping an open parasol from the top window of his house. When he dropped it with the handle downwards the parasol swung and oscillated violently on its journey to the ground, just as Garnerim's parachute had done. But when Cocking retrieved it and then dropped it out of the window with the handle *upwards*, it fell in a straight line without oscillating at all.

From this he reasoned that a parachute should be made like an 'upside-down umbrella', and when he finally constructed one it seems obvious that he never worked out any figures concerning his load, his area or the strength of materials at his command. Naturally, he needed a rigid framework, which he built out of three tubular hoops of different sizes, the biggest (at the top) being 107 feet round. These he trusted, one can only imagine by guesswork, to hold up against the supposed air pressure. The whole he covered with Irish linen, making an inverted cone of only just over 120 square yards surface. All this, together with a basket to sit in and his own weight, made up a load of over 400 pounds.

As might be expected, he had some difficulty in persuading any balloonist of the year 1837 to help him in his experiments. Even when he got the use of the Royal Vauxhall Nassau balloon, and arranged to make his ascent from the famous Vauxhall Gardens in London, the aeronauts who were to take him aloft refused to be responsible for his release. They insisted that he did this himself, and a device was fitted which he could work from the basket below and let the parachute fall free when he decided to do so.

The two aeronauts who took him up in the Nassau were Charles Green and Edward Spencer. The latter's descendants, by the way, became famous in the world of lighter-than-air craft as long as they remained in use in Europe. Neither the two balloonists nor the manager of the Vauxhall Gardens liked the idea of this contraption. On the day of the attempt they tried strongly to persuade him to give it up. But Cocking was as courageous as he was mistaken. He insisted upon the attempt and at last was lifted by the Nassau from the Gardens and carried to a height of 5000 feet, which he reckoned to be the best for the attempt.

By that time the balloon was floating between Blackheath and Greenwich. There was little wind and no low cloud. Then, from below the basket, Green and Spencer heard Cocking call out to them.

"Good night, Spencer," he shouted. "Good night, Green." Those were his last words. A moment later he had pulled the release and the inverted cone parachute dropped straight down. As the balloon naturally rose swiftly in the opposite direction, Green and Spencer leant over the side of their basket watching, badly troubled by the obvious speed of Cocking's fall. Then the inevitable happened. After falling very fast for several hundred feet, the 'upside-down umbrella' suddenly collapsed under the pressure and 'shut up'. Cocking, in his basket, fell headlong and finally crashed into a field close by the village of Lee Green, where he died shortly after he was found. He now lies in the churchyard.

But if poor, brave Cocking threw his life away, he at least demonstrated to future experimenters that careful calculation of known forces and stresses was necessary to any form of aircraft design. Nevertheless, scores of men in the years that followed repeated Cocking's mistakes or copied, badly, the methods of Garnerim. There were fatalities and there were successes. But the first flexible silk canopy which could be folded and stowed was invented by the late Major Thomas Baldwin, an American who also built the first airship to fly in that country. When he died in 1923 at the ripe age of seventy-three he had amassed a fortune of over a million dollars.

All previous man-carrying parachutes, by whatever means they were opened, had been rigid—that is, they had either hoops or ribs to stretch their canopies when they were inflated. This, for obvious reasons, made their use with aeroplanes impossible. Baldwin was followed by the Italian G. A. Farini, who also invented a flexible parachute; but both these were of the type which are attached to the aircraft, and not 'freely' attached to the man.

During the First World War, a brilliant British designer, E. R. Chalrop, designed the 'Guardian Angel' type, and an almost identical type during the same period was made by the German, Heinecke. In both these designs the parachute was for the first time fixed to the airman, but it was not 'free' in the full sense of the word. There was a line attached to the aircraft which yanked the parachute out of its container as the airman jumped.

The principle that there must be some attachment between the falling man and the aircraft in order to open the parachute was a feature of all the designs I have mentioned. The idea, of course, was to ensure that the parachute *would* open; the surest method of doing it was to use the airman's falling weight.

Although this represented safety in one way, however, it was also a deadly danger in another. The danger was that the 'safety line' would become entangled with the aircraft itself, when it was diving or spinning, and thus drag the airman down to death whether the parachute had opened or not. There was also the problem of growing speeds. As aircraft became faster—and they were soon capable of travelling very much faster on the level than a man does when he falls—there was the risk of a suddenly-opened parachute being burst and ripped apart by the force of the wind.

Meanwhile, the war of 1914–18 had been fought out at a terrific cost in the lives of courageous and highly trained pilots and crews, since there was no completely free type of parachute with which they could get out when their machines had been shot up or were in flames.

When the war came to an end, therefore, all men who still flew fast aircraft, whether in the way of service or civilian life, were waiting for some inventor who could give them a chance of survival when the worst happened to their machines.

That man was ready. He was still only a youngster, born in Los Angeles, California, but he had spent his life since schooldays building parachute models—and then real parachutes, and finally a free parachute in which he had full confidence. That youngster's name was Leslie Irvin.

The reason why more than 40000 men can thank Leslie Irvin for their lives has its inception in a fire balloon he was taken to watch at Chutes Park, Los Angeles, when he was ten years old. The balloon rose because the air inside it was heated by a lump of flaming tow held on a grid stretched across its lower opening. After the tow had burnt out, the balloon still went on rising until the air inside it cooled down. Then it started to fall. This suggested to young Irvin's ingenious mind the perfect way to test the parachutes he had already been making with any odd bits of silk his mother would let him have.

At that time, the year 1910, the aircraft driven by the petrol engine was an accomplished fact. Irvin was reading everything he could possibly lay his hands on about aeroplanes, balloons, airships or indeed anything that could be made to fly. Why the parachute in itself had always fascinated him so tremendously he could never definitely say. But not long afterwards he built a fire balloon strong enough to carry the family cat, in a harness, high into the air. Naturally enough, when the fire had burnt out and the air inside the balloon cooled, down came the cat, fast. But this is where young Irvin's ingenious idea worked. A carefully-made parachute had been attached to the cat's harness. When the animal was falling fast enough the parachute inflated. The cat, swinging safely upon it, landed gently without even one of its nine lives having been forfeit.

One day during his teens the young experimenter came upon a group of men who were building a primitive aeroplane in a field near his home. This was a heaven-sent chance, and Irvin spent every minute of his free hours, or when he could play hookey from school, hanging around them and trying to make himself useful. Sometime later, the leader of the group, a man named Gil Dosh, actually offered him a job. Although this meant him giving up his last year or so at school, he raced home to badger his mother and father until at last they let him have his way.

The aeroplane he helped Gil Dosh to build not only flew when it was completed but was the first aeroplane ever to be seen over the city of Los Angeles, and one of the first to be used commercially, since it made a flight between there and San Bernadino and returned with a delivery of newspapers.

For the next few years young Irvin moved on from job to job and only once took employment which was not actually connected with flying. He worked with the famous pilot, Lincoln Beachy, who used to give shows flying low over track-driver Barney Oldfield and racing him. Irvin moved on to a job with Roy Knabenshue, who had built one of the early dirigible airships and was plying it for hire (not very profitably) in the Los Angeles district. Then, in a hard-up period, he had to take his one 'ground' job with the old Universal Film Company in their employment office. But even in that he did not entirely stay out of the air. On more than one occasion the Company needed an airman for stunting in one of their films, and by virtue of his position, Irvin gave himself the job.

As far as records go it seems that the famous French airman Pegoud (the first man to loop the loop) and young Irvin were the first men in the history of aviation to parachute from aeroplanes. At that time most pilots feared that if a passenger suddenly jumped out of an aeroplane, the loss of his weight would put it out of control and might overturn it. Irvin had for a long time been trying to break down this prejudice, but the pilots he met weren't convinced. Then to his delight he saw in the newspapers one day that someone in Venice, California, was offering a considerable money prize for the first man who would try such a descent. Irvin put in for the prize forthwith. The pilot hired for the job was still afraid of the violent alteration of control that might be caused by anyone jumping from a rear seat, so Irvin went up sitting on the axle between the wheels of the undercarriage.

The parachute he used then was not a 'free' one. It was a flexible canopy stowed in a sack fixed to the bottom of the cockpit. When he reckoned that he had a good, safe height to play with, Irvin left the undercarriage axle and dropped straight down. He had a line attached to his body which jerked the canopy out of the sack. Not only did the canopy open safely but the pilot found no difficulty in controlling the aircraft, which merely nosed up into a gentle climb directly after Irvin had gone away.

That exploit gained him the name of 'Ski-Hi' and a good deal of publicity, but flying was then only in its infancy and there was not much money to be made out of it. Irvin wandered about America getting jobs where he could, flying whenever possible, whether for money or not, and still obsessed by his idea of the safe 'free' parachute. He took jobs in carnivals and kept himself going by playing the piano for the dancers. He worked as a hypnotist's stooge and finally found that the best-paid job in the outfit was that of a high diver. Soon he was going off heights of 70 feet for the edification of the crowds, and it was while he was doing this that he found the answer to a problem which had been worrying the highest officers of the air forces of the world.

By now it had become obvious that a 'free' parachute was the only type which could be used by men who had to leave their aircraft in war. There must be no line attached which could foul up in any way with a spinning machine. But this meant that the opening of the parachute must be left to the man who jumped. And no one had yet discovered how far a man could fall headlong from a great height without losing consciousness.

There were high and solemn medical authorities who announced that no man could fall more than a few hundred feet without passing out. They supplied learned and complicated reasons for their statements. Even today, amongst non-flying people, you will hear it said of any kind of accident involving a long fall: 'Poor man, how dreadful; but of course he must have fainted long before he hit the ground.'

Young Leslie Irvin had never believed in this or in any of the scientific reasons given by the top-hatted medical personages. Cutting out all the jargon, he could see no good or sufficient reason why a man *should* faint when falling, unless of course it might be from pure fright. And he did not believe in being frightened.

In the course of his high-diving job, therefore, he was very careful to make an exact check of his senses and sensations from the moment he left his 70-foot-high diving board until he entered the water. Since he was perfectly confident of his own skill in diving, he found that he remained absolutely in command of all his senses during the long drop to the water. In fact, he convinced himself of what has subsequently been proved, that the effect of falling, in itself, has no effect on a healthy man no matter how far he drops. This is largely because no man of average weight and bulk can fall faster than about 120 miles an hour. When he reaches that speed the normal air pressure against his body prevents his falling any faster, and he simply goes on at 120 miles an hour until his parachute opens or, in less fortunate cases, until he strikes the earth.

It was not until the year 1919, however, that Irvin found the chance to demonstrate the theories he had been building up in his mind. Meanwhile, he scraped and saved his money, launched himself as a stunt parachutist in his own right, and toured the country. But at that time he could not afford to make the free type of parachute he had in mind with all the gear that would make it spring open when he pulled the release. As a stunt man he used what was to hand—the pull-out type, the container of which was attached to the aircraft. Still his stunting, although nothing much more than a highly courageous circus act, stood him in good stead. When the time came for the authorities to look around for men who knew about parachuting, Irvin had made so many jumps that they had to take him seriously.

The main authority in America considering the matter at that time was Major E. J. Hoffman, who had been empowered to try to find a workable type of free parachute, together with a man who would demonstrate it. He had gathered together a panel of experts who, for many months, examined and tested every known design. At last the panel issued a list of conditions which had to be satisfied by any designer who asked for consideration. The conditions were tough, as they had need to be. Every possibility of failure, as far as the expert panel could contrive, was eliminated by the conditions they set.

The design which young Irvin immediately sent in was the only one which satisfied almost all the conditions demanded. It was accepted, the parachute was made, and then came the momentous question of actual test. Typically, Irvin demanded that he himself be allowed to make the first test of his invention. In spite of misgivings, Major Hoffman agreed.

It will be remembered that no man had so far attempted a free fall during which he was relying on his own possession of his faculties and his courage so that he could open his own parachute during the drop. Moreover, some medical pundits were still saying that a man, falling freely, would lose his senses before he could operate the release mechanism.

There was, as yet, no actual proof that the dismal doctors were talking nonsense, and Hoffman and his band of experts were feeling far from happy on the morning of April 28th, 1919, for which the test was scheduled. As they walked out on to Dayton Airfield, Leslie Irvin was ready and waiting with his new parachute strapped to his body. He shook hands all round, noted the white faces, and grinned inwardly because he realized that he was the only man present who was not frightened.

Then he climbed up on to an aircraft piloted by his old friend Floyd Smith (whose parachute theories had always been the same as his own) and the engine was started. Smith took off, made a wide circle of the area while gaining height, and then came back to fly directly across the field at around 2000 feet.

On the ground there was dead silence among the group of watchers, each of whom feared that he was probably going to witness an unpleasant tragedy. High above, Irvin looked down and saw the bunch of white faces concentrating upon him. He turned and grinned at Smith, gave him a cheerful wave of a hand—and then dived.

For a few seconds nobody on the ground saw his movement. Then someone yelled : "There he is !", and there was a general gasp as the tiny silhouette of his figure was seen somersaulting down the sky behind the aircraft.

Irvin fell head over heels for 200 feet, for 300, and went on falling. Among the group on the airfield a man croaked: "My God, he's fainted. He'll be killed."

Major Hoffman's throat was dry. Irvin fell 400 feet—500. It seemed that the doctors had been right after all. A grim tragedy threatened to be the ending of months of careful work and scheming. Then, when he had fallen more than 600 feet, a flutter of white silk was seen breaking out above Irvin's plummeting body. The silk spread out above him, turned into a spreading mushroom, and a few seconds later he was swinging gently on his open parachute, coming down securely and comfortably to land without a bruise as the yelling group of delighted experts raced towards him across the airfield.

Leslie Irvin achieved three things by that one descent. He was the first man in history to make a 'delayed release' jump. He was the first man to prove that a free fall of hundreds of feet does *not* make a man lose consciousness; he had deliberately dropped a third of the distance to demonstrate the fact. He was the first man to jump in a free-type parachute.

. . . . .

Irvin's free-type parachute was immediately adopted by the American Air Force, by the RAF and later by most of the air forces of the world. Other fine designs by various makers have been adopted since then, but it is Leslie Irvin who holds pride of place as pioneer, and the products of his firm are still standard service equipment.

Irvin, however, is not a member of his own Caterpillar Club. This is because he has never been forced to bale out of an aircraft or die, in spite of the fact that he has jumped over 300 times in the course of testing his own invention.

Another paradox is the fact that the first man admitted to the Caterpillar Club also did not bale out of a doomed aircraft. But since the Irvin parachute he was wearing saved his life, he was granted the badge. The circumstances of this descent are unique.

On August 24th, 1920, at Dayton Airfield, a Mr O'Connor made a jump to demonstrate a different kind of parachute. The authorities, however, feared for his life and insisted that he wore an Irvin pack as well, a demand that angered O'Connor, but for which he had cause to be devoutly thankful within the next half-hour.

After baling out at 2000 feet O'Connor jerked the release of the new-type parachute he had come to demonstrate—but nothing happened. He tried again, and yet again, until he had fallen to within 500 feet of the ground. Then he desperately wrenched at the release-ring of his Irvin, which opened forthwith, and carried him down to a safe landing.

It is understood that Mr O'Connor thereafter always wore braces as well as a belt.

. . . . .

The first Service member of the Caterpillar Club joined just over two years after Irvin's demonstration. And about seven months later all American military airmen were ordered to wear the parachute every time they flew.

Lieutenant Harold R. Harris, a pilot of long experience, was testing a Leoning aircraft to mark its behaviour with a new design of balanced ailerons. For a while he practised turns, dives and climbs and was not altogether satisfied with the characteristics of the machine. However, he had no reason to suspect any radical fault and when, at about 2500 feet, he spotted another aircraft which he knew was being flown by Lieutenant Fairchild, a comrade, he decided to have a spot of fun.

In the way that thousands of spirited young pilots have done, and will always do, Harris dived on his friend, inviting him to a fight. Fairchild accepted the invitation and made his first evasive action by a diving turn, then swerving away in the opposite direction. Harris, however, came round, hard on his heels, holding him in his gun ring-sight. Speeds in those days sound faintly comic to the 600-plus-mile-an-hour jet boys of our H-bomb age. Harris saw that he was doing 150, which was as fast as most fighter-pilots had travelled at the time. In fact, by his standards he was going like a ding-bat; the fight was on, the vast blue bowl of the sky a playground for any exponents of whizz.

Still, 150 miles an hour in any age and time is fast enough when an aircraft decides to come apart. Harris, in a tight climbing turn after his foe, suddenly felt a terrific vibration from the wings. Instinctively he levelled off, the machine answering sluggishly and drunkenly to the lateral control. Then, as he throttled back, he saw large areas of fabric splitting and flying back off the left wing.

In that same moment the control column wrenched itself out of his hand and began to thresh wildly round the cockpit. He grabbed for it again but got such a crack across the back of his right hand that he feared the bones had been broken even through the leather of his glove. Out of the tail of his eye he noticed that the left aileron was stuck upright, almost at right angles to the disintegrating wing. Meanwhile, the control stick was battering at his knees while the aircraft lurched over to the left and plunged earthwards in a screaming 200-mph dive.

With bits of the left wing collapsing and flying off past his head, Harris flicked undone his safety-belt and thrust himself up out of the cockpit. Even in those hectic few moments he had decided that he must get his feet braced against the side of the machine and kick himself away as hard as he could. That didn't prove necessary. To his astonishment, he suddenly found himself apparently floating in mid-air while the aircraft plunged downwards beneath. The fierce 200-mph rush of air had lifted him clear before he knew it.

He realized that the falling aircraft had entirely disappeared and there was nothing but blue sky beneath his feet. Almost at the same moment the earth-horizon appeared at a crazy angle and swept below him again. He realized that he was falling head over heels in somersaults.

Harris grabbed for the rip-cord ring and gave it a hearty wrench. He waited for the canopy to open and wondered what the jerk would be like. Nothing happened. He wrenched again, with the uncomfortable feeling that his heart had wedged between his back teeth, because he felt no movement that would indicate that the pack behind him had opened. He pulled a third time with all his might, the force of the action causing his body to spin as well as somersault in a flying whirl of arms and legs.

It was this contortion which actually saved him. He caught sight of his own hand and saw that he had been pulling uselessly at one of the harness-webs instead of the parachute release-ring. With understandable briskness he corrected the little mistake, finding to his vast relief that the ring needed only a light pull to make the pack snap open. Still turning head over heels he saw the lines stream out and the big, silken canopy break out and spread in the sunshine.

Although afterwards he could never remember whether there had been any jerk or not, he had the blessed sensation of finding that he was firmly and safely supported. The somersaulting had stopped and he was floating gently towards a bank of bushes near a couple of isolated houses. But, as Fairchild in the other aircraft was able to testify, Harris had fallen a clear 1800 feet before he opened his pack—thus adding the second 'delayed drop' to his distinction of being the first man to save his life in an enforced bale-out in the free type of parachute.

As he finally landed, without injury, he saw his aircraft crash with tremendous impact into open ground a few hundred yards away, and explode in a tower of flame.

3

FOUR TIMES LUCKY

CHARLES A. LINDBERGH flew the Atlantic Ocean, alone, from New York to Paris direct, in May 1927. This ocean had already been flown twice. An American naval crew were the first across but they did it in a series of 'hops', via the Azores.

The first non-stop flight was made by the British RAF officers John Alcock and Arthur Whitten-Brown, both of whom were subsequently knighted. They made the crossing in a Vickers-Vimy-Rolls bomber aircraft in one hop from Newfoundland to Ireland.

Lindbergh's flight, however, caught the imagination of the whole world because it was the first solo crossing, and because he went from one capital city direct to the other. There was also the important fact that he proved to be utterly different from the popular idea of an American. He was modest, quiet, refused to engage in any personal ballyhoo, and had a deep charm of manner which endeared him to everyone he met.

It was typical of him that during all the acclamations and the Press interviews that followed he made no mention of another personal distinction which was, at that time, unique. No one heard then, and few have heard since, that Charles Lindbergh was Boss Caterpillar even before he made his Atlantic flight, with four parachute jumps from doomed aircraft to his credit.

Lindbergh took to his parachute for the first time when he was a cadet in the United States Army Air Service at Kelly Field, Texas, in 1924. On this occasion he was pilot of one of a formation of nine SE5 single-seater fighter aircraft which had been detailed to carry out diving attacks upon a De Havilland 4B flying at 4000 feet, a few hundred feet above a cloud layer.

The formation, as usual, was flying in three vics (vee-formation) of three aircraft. Lindbergh was flying on the left-hand side of his own vic with Cadet Love leading, and Lieutenant McAllister on the right. The orders were for the leader of each vic to attack and then climb away swiftly. His wing men would then attack in their turn and climb away in the same direction their leader had taken to re-form with him and carry on.

Accordingly, Cadet Love made his attack on the De Havilland, fired his camera guns and climbed away. Lindbergh then attacked from his left-hand position, thinking he would be followed by McAllister from the right. Lindbergh recalls that after Cadet Love pulled up there was no other aircraft nearby. Lindbergh passed above the De Havilland in the course of his attack, and a moment later felt a slight jolt followed by a crash. His head was thrown forward against the cowling of his plane and for an instant he seemed to hang nearly motionless. He closed his throttle and saw Lieutenant McAllister in his cockpit a few feet to his left. The aircraft were locked together with the fuselages approximately parallel.

What had actually happened was that McAllister had lagged in his dive. Lindbergh had gone beneath him to make his attack, but in climbing away sharply he brought his aircraft up under the one McAllister was flying, and crashed into it from below.

The right upper wing of Lindbergh's biplane smashed into McAllister's left lower wing, into which his whirling propeller ploughed its way, sending up a terrific spray of shattered spars and fragments before breaking off short. Since the aircraft were both going in the same direction and only on slightly different climbing angles, the force of the collision was comparatively slight. Both cockpits were undamaged but the two machines were solidly locked together. In that position they heaved over and began plunging down the sky in a spin.

Half-dazed from the heavy blow on his head, Lindbergh unclipped his safety-belt and pushed himself up in the cockpit. But then the damaged left top wing began flapping and vibrating wildly . . . banging him on the head with each movement. He wriggled sideways, feeling rather as though he were being beaten up by a gang of toughs, but managed to slide out of the cockpit, which he realized was in almost a vertical position as the two aircraft whirled down the sky. Somehow he got his feet on the cockpit edge and then sprang clean off backwards, trying to put himself as far from the wrecked aircraft as possible.

It seemed to him that the tangled wreck was falling nearly straight down, and for some time he fell in line with it and only slightly to one side. He didn't want to risk it fouling the opening parachute, so delayed pulling the rip-cord. He turned head over heels one and a half times and was falling flat on his face as he went into cloud. Then he thought it better to pull the ring, which he did, and the parachute functioned perfectly. Coming out of cloud he saw Lieutenant McAllister floating down above him also on his parachute. The wrecked planes went past about a hundred yards to one side, still spinning to the right and leaving a trail of fragments. Lindbergh watched them until, still locked together, they crashed into the mesquite about 2000 feet below. Several seconds after they had hit the ground they burst into flame.

Lieutenant McAllister's report of the incident followed that of Lindbergh in all respects—except, of course, in the details of his own jump. He recalled that they were in cloud when he jumped and as near as he could tell the planes were going down in a left spiral. He dived clear over the right side of the fuselage and slightly to the rear. The business of counting three before pulling the ring never entered his head. He pulled the ring right away and the parachute opened immediately. Lindbergh was below him in his parachute and off to one side. On landing they found that someone had put a nice soft ploughed field underneath. That was something to appreciate in view of the fact that there was nothing but mesquite everywhere else for miles around.

Both men landed unhurt. The cause of the accident was a dual fault, one of those inexplicable things that must occur from time to time in flying. Lindbergh had been wrong in the direction he took when pulling out from his attack on the De Havilland. McAllister had been at fault in delaying the speed of his dive. He, of course, was the only eye-witness of all that happened since he was in the upper of the two fighters. He saw Lindbergh's SE5 banking and rising up directly beneath him. He saw that Lindbergh's head was likely to crash straight into his whirling propeller, and wrenched his machine into a climbing turn to try and save the other's life. But since Lindbergh was going faster as the result of his dive and could therefore climb more steeply, the collision was inevitable.

It was typical of young Lindbergh, however, that after he had landed and compared notes with McAllister he was far more worried about the loss of his goggles and vest-pocket camera, which had disappeared during his bale-out.

Lindbergh made his second jump only about three months after the first. This time a new aircraft which he was testing as a Lieutenant in the Air Corps Reserve broke up under him, and he got out when he was estimated to be less than 300 feet from the ground. This was at the Lambert, St Louis Field, which was the station of the 35th Divisional Air Service. From that point he lived what was, for him, a peaceful existence for well over another year. Then in the space of only three weeks he had to take to his parachute twice more.

These two jumps were in almost identical circumstances (with the exception of one factor), so I will only detail the first of them, which was Number Three in his total of four leaps.

By September 1926 Lindbergh had achieved one of his life's ambitions. He had become an airmail pilot, flying on the St Louis–Chicago run. At this time he had left the Reserve, but had joined the Missouri National Guard. On the afternoon of the 16th of that month he took off with a load of mail on board at 4.25 pm and touched down by schedule at Springfield and at Peoria, leaving the latter city at 6.10, setting the normal course north-east.

At that time the sky was clear with only scattered clouds in the heights. There was a slight ground haze but nothing to worry Lindbergh, who continued course in the twilight and flew by his compass as darkness fell, checking his route by the lights of the towns below. But when he was a few miles north-east of Marseilles and the Illinois River, a thick fog began rolling in underneath him. Lindbergh found the top of the fog at about 600 feet. He flew through it for a while, gently losing height, but soon realized that if it did not extend right down to the ground it certainly went far too low for him to investigate any further.

Therefore he climbed out of it again and turned back along his course. Where he thought the fog was thinner, he dropped a flare, hoping that he could circle round it and see clearly enough by its light to land. But the flare did not work, and Lindbergh had to head for Maywood hoping that he might find a chance of scraping down at the airfield there.

Since he was later to prove by his ocean crossings that he was one of the greatest aerial navigators who have ever flown, it is not surprising that throughout all this Lindbergh kept an accurate check of his compass course. After a while he saw a glow through the fog which showed that a town was below. He realized there were several glowing patches showing vaguely through the fog but could only spot them when looking away from the bright moon which was hanging in the clear sky above. These he knew to be towns lying around the airfield at Maywood, but although he strained his eyes through the vagueness he could not find any indication of where the field actually lay, and this was in spite of the fact (as he learned later) that the airfield's searchlights had been switched on and turned up to guide him when his engine was heard droning overhead. In addition two barrels of gasolene had been set alight.

Lindbergh circled the Maywood district for 35 minutes. By then it was after eight and he knew that his fuel would only carry him on until 9.30 pm. For this reason he took a course due west to make quite sure that he was well clear of Lake Michigan. Then he turned south-west again knowing he would be on the line of the Illinois River, and hoping to see it if he reached the end of the fog-bank or found that it thinned.

At 8.20 pm his engine cut. Lindbergh immediately switched on his reserve tank but the engine refused to pick up. What had happened he didn't know, but since his height was now only 1500 feet the situation was desperate. He grabbed a flashlight and pushed it into his belt. He was about to release his parachute flare and go over the side, when the engine coughed, fired jerkily for a few revolutions, and then began to run as sweetly as before.

Knowing that he was now running only on his reserve tank, and only a short while was left in hand before it ran dry, he realized that baling out would be inevitable, since there was no sign of any thinning in the fog below. He therefore tried to open the mail compartment in the hope that he could throw the mail-sacks over the side before he jumped himself. This would at least prevent them from being burned when the aircraft finally crashed. However, he couldn't get the compartment open. Therefore he decided to climb, steering the aircraft well away from any glow that denoted a town, and go on climbing until the reserve tank ran dry.

When he reached 5000 feet the engine spluttered and died again. Since there was nothing further he could do, Lindbergh unclipped his safety-belt, slid over the side and dropped away into the darkness. After what he judged to be about a 100-foot fall he pulled the rip-cord, and almost immediately the parachute opened above him and jerked him upright in his harness. Then he pulled the flashlight from his belt and shone it down towards the top of the fog-bank.

Whereupon there was an unpleasant sound. He heard the engine of his aircraft suddenly pick up again and start running, close at hand. Then he actually saw the machine, about a quarter of a mile away in the clear moonlight. It was flying level and heading directly towards him as he hung helplessly beneath his parachute.

Lindbergh slammed his flashlight into his pocket and grabbed the shroud lines to pull on them with all his strength in the hope of side-slipping out of the way of the oncoming aircraft. Whether he managed to alter direction much or not, he never afterwards knew. As it was, the aircraft passed him at the same level and a distance of about 300 yards, and he saw that it was in a gently diving spiral.

It was then that he realized what had happened. When the engine finally cut at 5000 feet he had been certain that the reserve tank was dry. Therefore he had not bothered to switch off the ignition. What he had forgotten, of course, was the fact that there would be a gallon or so of fuel left in the tank, but owing to the angle of climb it had not reached the carburettor feed-line. Once he had left the aircraft and it had taken up its natural gliding angle, with the nose down, the petrol slopped back into the feed-line . . . and the still-switched-on engine naturally started to run again.

Meanwhile, the aircraft still droned close at hand.

Suddenly he saw it a second time swinging round and coming towards him. By now, however, he realized that he was in the centre of the spiral path it was following, so there was hope that it might not fly directly into him or his parachute. Nevertheless, with the vagaries of the wind—which he could not judge—and a dozen other possible factors that might alter the machine's course, his position was distinctly uncomfortable.

On this parachute journey down to the top of the fog-bank, Lndbergh counted five separate spirals that the machine made round him, but each time he was relieved to see that it was just a little further away. Then, when he found himself dropping into the clammy blackness of the fog, he grabbed for his flashlight . . . but found it missing. He could see absolutely nothing. He did not even know whether he was penduluming on his parachute harness. All he knew was that he must be a great deal less than 1000 feet from the ground, so he crossed his legs to make sure he would not straddle a tree branch or an electric wire, put his hands over his face, and waited.

With a heavy thud he found himself rolling over and over with a peculiar rustling sound around him. He staggered to his feet and found himself in quite clear visibility in the middle of a cornfield, with the fog-bank 50 feet or so above his head.

Lindbergh gathered his parachute, made his way to a nearby farm, and persuaded the farmer to get out his car and help him look for the aircraft, which he knew must by that time have crashed. Eventually they found it about two miles away, surrounded by the inhabitants of another farmhouse which it had narrowly missed.

His report of the incident was typically terse, and concerned with the only matter which he felt that an airmail pilot should bother about: 'The aircraft had come to rest at the edge of a cornfield without causing any casualties. The mail compartment was broken open and one sack of mail was on the ground. None of the mail, however, was damaged or missing.'

4

DESERT SECRET

WAR is a mysterious business in many ways. To all civilized people it is a mystery how war can be started by anyone, even a power-drunk, melancholic lunatic. It is even more mysterious how such a dangerous imbecile can gain autocratic power over millions of his countrymen . . . and then manage to conjure up all their most primitive instincts of hate and vicious cruelty. Problems of this magnitude must be for future historians to explain.

The story I am about to record here concerns only one man, a certain Flying Officer Mackenzie of the Royal New Zealand Air Force, but it remains one of the most puzzling mysteries of the entire war. I shall set out the sequence of events exactly in the order they took place.

In the spring of 1941 Mackenzie was one of the pilots of 14 Squadron, at that time operating from landing ground No21, which lay east of Mersa Matruh in the Western Desert. The Squadron was equipped with twin-engined Blenheims, excellent aircraft in their day, but at this period of the war outclassed by most of the machines operated by the enemy. Naturally, however, the Squadron did not allow this difference to have the slightest effect on the prosecution of their little corner of the fight. They merely set to work in the traditional way to get the best possible, and a bit more, out of the aircraft they were flying. This, generally speaking, meant that they flew as close as possible to the Blenheim's endurance.

They kept up highly offensive attacks upon targets which the enemy thought they couldn't normally reach. This usually involved scraping home with only a last gallon or two slopping around in the tanks.

On May 26th, Flying Officer Mackenzie, Sergeant McConnell, his wireless operator-gunner, and Sergeant Fearn, his observer, were detailed as crew of one of three Blenheims which were to fly to the island of Crete and there bomb concentrations of enemy troops on a stretch of ground which lay between Suda Bay and Maleme. All three crews knew perfectly well that this was a 'limit of endurance' run. They had absolutely nothing in reserve. Only if they made a straight track to their target, dropped their bombs quickly as well as accurately, and made a straight track back, was there any hope of getting home. There was leeway neither for bad luck nor 'finger trouble'.

The three aircraft took off on time and got on with the job. Mackenzie was flying in number two position behind the right wing of the leader. He had not been flying long when he saw that his opposite number to the left was having trouble. A haze of smoke was coming from the exhaust of one of number three's engines and, as it began dropping back from the formation, the affected engine slowed so that the propeller blades became visible. Soon it was getting left well behind and losing height. Therefore, when Fearn reported that it had turned and was making back for base, nobody blamed the pilot. On an endurance run of this kind, when nothing can be left to chance, a man is only doing his duty in taking a dud engine home.

After that the remaining two aircraft carried straight on and droned out over the Mediterranean. The crews bore the tedium in their various ways until at last the island of Crete hove in sight. Both the leading observer and Fearn, in Mackenzie's aircraft, had their objective firmly pin-pointed. They roared over Suda Bay and then, as the troop concentrations were spotted, went into the attack.

Fearn and McConnell felt they had done a good job when, five minutes later, they swung away out of a hail of flak with all bombs gone. The pilots of both aircraft had pressed the attack home spiritedly in spite of fierce counter-attack. Now, at the extreme point of their outward limit of flying, there was no time for more detailed observation of the results. Their duty—just as much as their inclination—was to turn and take as straight a course for base as was possible.

Fortunately, both aircraft appeared to be intact and none of the crews had been hit. But soon after they flew out over the ocean again, twilight began closing in, and with the swift change that is usual in the tropics, the horizon disappeared and the sky became completely dark.

At that time and in that theatre of war there were no long-distance radio-aids to pilots. Mackenzie's leader, therefore, could only fly homeward on a compass course. And Mackenzie himself could only keep his position in close formation by carefully watching his leader's station-keeping light.

Both crews, however, were quite cheerful. The job had been a hot one while it lasted and they knew that they had been lucky to get away without damage to themselves or their aircraft. As to the immediate future, there was no reason to suppose that good navigation would fail to get them back over base at the appointed time. Then their landing would be a matter of routine.

Nevertheless, it was a long, lonely run and as time spun out Mackenzie began glancing at his petrol gauges. By all rules and regulations he knew that they should be approaching base pretty soon, but whether he was over the sea or land he had no means of knowing. Everything had gone well and the engines were running as sweetly as he could have wished. But the gauges showed that he could not keep his aircraft in the air much longer.

He was relieved to see the light on the leading aircraft go down the sky. Naturally enough, he and his crew imagined that the leader had spotted base and was swinging down the sky to pick up the airstrip, and land. Mackenzie therefore brought his aircraft down to a couple of thousand feet.

Then, to their horror, the crew saw a brilliant flash from below. It only lasted a second, but its meaning was evident. The landing aircraft had hit something—and exploded. Presumably the leader had gone into ground, but there was no actual evidence whether he had struck land or water.

In that crash, as it afterwards transpired, all three of the crew were killed instantly. During the long flight home, the leader had got off course. Whether he misjudged his height when flying low, or whether he was trying to make a landing, will never be known. Whatever it was, the luck was against him. His aircraft struck the edge of the Qattara Depression—a vast, sunken plateau in the desert, edged by a sheer cliff—a formation that looks like a gigantic fault or join in the surface of the earth.

Mackenzie had no means of knowing this at the time. He could only fly straight ahead on the same course, and leave the wireless operator to do what he could to fix position. Neither he nor his observer had been able to check details of their path through the darkness up to now. As was natural, they had relied on the leader. They realized that they were lost. They had no idea of the direction of their base, and petrol was perilously low.

Mackenzie did not know he was anywhere near the Qattara Depression, or even over land. The flash had not been sufficient for him to see any surrounding detail clearly.

He ordered McConnell to try to get a bearing from any mobile D/F unit that might be around. McConnell reported that he had been trying just that ever since the leading aircraft crashed, but he wasn't getting any joy.

"Well, let's face it, I don't know where we are," Mackenzie said to Fearn. "I can only suppose he hit land and not water when he blew up. The flash was so short I saw no surroundings."

"That goes for me too, sir," said Fearn, grimly.

Mackenzie came to a decision. "It's no good trying to scrape down and make a landing—if we *are* over land—chaps," he said quietly. "It's fifty to one we'd go in just like the other poor devils. I'll take her up with what petrol we've got left, and we'll just have to jump for it, that's all."

"We ought to try to keep together," said Fearn, "but by the time we've got out of the kite in our turns, we'll probably land half a mile apart, and we won't be able to see each other in this darkness."

"Well, we'll see the aircraft when she goes in," said Mackenzie, pulling up into a climb. "She'll burn and we'll see her clearly enough. Each of us must mark the burning wreckage. When we land all we've got to do is to walk towards it. That way we're bound to meet."

"Suppose one of us busts a leg, or anything like that, getting dragged by a parachue?" asked McConnell.

Mackenzie shrugged. "If anyone does that, well, just let him lie still where he is. Let him get his parachute spread well out on the ground if he can manage to do so, but otherwise he's to remain just where he falls, and not move. Then the other two are pretty well bound to find him when there's enough light to see, after dawn."

Since the plan seemed to be as good as any could be in the circumstances, no one said any more until one of the engines started to run unevenly, showing that the tanks were practically bone dry.

"All right, bale out," snapped Mackenzie. "Come on, McConnell, you first."

McConnell felt across his parachute harness, made sure

that the clips were in place and then, with his teeth set, went out head first. Before he had counted the regulation number and jerked his release ring, the aircraft had disappeared entirely in the darkness. But, as his parachute opened, he heard the drone of the Blenheim's remaining engine cough and falter into silence. By that time, at Mackenzie's order, Fearn, the observer, had also jumped. He, too, was brought up with a comforting jerk as his parachute opened.

But from that moment onwards neither of the two sergeants, nor any other living man, ever saw or heard of Mackenzie again.

. . . . .

Fearn and McConnell drifted down on their parachutes, as Mackenzie had foreseen, at a probable distance of about half a mile apart. They could see nothing above them and nothing below. Naturally, they could not see each other, nor had they any means of knowing whether their pilot had baled out or not.

Then the worst happened. There was a sudden vivid explosion from below. For one instant both saw a mass of wreckage as the aircraft they had left crashed headlong into the scrub. But, as in the case of the leader's aircraft, there was just one explosion. The crash did not take fire.

Aircraft are freakish things and these single explosions may have been caused by the fact that there was no petrol, but only inflammable gas left within the aircraft tanks. In any case the flickering blaze they had hoped for, which would have given them a meeting-point, just didn't happen. After that one explosion the darkness closed in like velvet. And when each man had dropped into the sand, released himself from his parachute, and then got up, there was nothing whatever to give him an idea as to which way to walk.

The two sergeants tried shouting and hallooing . . .

and then listening breathlessly. But they were too far apart to hear each other. Added to this, the stars were obscured and, until the early glow of the sun heralded the dawn, they could have no idea of north, south, east or west. Their only hope was that they were already overdue at their home base and a search would be laid on for them pretty soon.

In this their hopes were justified but, since they were much further away from base than they imagined, rescue was delayed for an almost fatal period. Searching aircraft were dispatched from landing ground No21 at dawn, but by noon they returned reporting no sign of either crash or survivors in spite of an intensive low-level quartering of the ground all about the area. Meanwhile, as has been mentioned before, 14 Squadron were occupied with a war, and very intensely occupied at that. They could not afford to let aircraft spend time in searching while there was the enemy to deal with. Group Headquarters was notified, therefore, and a big Bombay troop-carrier sent out to take over the rescue attempt.

For the next two days the Bombay searched from dawn to dusk. Towards the end of the third day Mackenzie's crashed Blenheim was found near the edge of the Qattarra Depression. The Bombay came down to land, the pilot looking carefully for 'brown' sand because the lighter colour indicates drift stuff into which the wheels of a heavy aircraft will sink and wreck the machine. The members of the search party tumbled out and examined the crash carefully in the blazing heat of the sun. But they found none of the crew, living or dead.

What they did find, about a mile away, forms the major part of this grim tale of mystery. Not far from a rough desert track, they spotted a parachute lying on the sand. To their astonishment they saw that the cords of the parachute had been cut clean through, obviously by a knife. A little further away was a broken stick. A careful examination showed that what seemed like half-obliterated footprints of a lame man led from the scene of the crash to where the parachute and the cut cords were lying.

Other than these extraordinary clues there was nothing to show what had happened to any of the men who had been flying in the aircraft.

The search all over the crash area was then intensified, but it was not until the sixth day that the first survivor was sighted. He was staggering drunkenly across the desert, miles to the north of the point where the aircraft had gone in. His face and body were so hideously covered with insect bites that at first he was unrecognizable, but in a croaking voice he was able to give his name . . . Sergeant Fearn, the observer.

At once he was hurried into the shade beneath the wing of the Bombay, washed down and attended to by the doctor who was with the search party, and then loaded on board and was taken back to base. Although he was suffering from exhaustion and thirst, he had managed to make fairly good going. In his search for water he had dug, with his bare hands, into the sand beneath scrub patches. When he found it he had had the good common sense to fill his Mae West. During the fierce heat of the days he had lain hidden in the scrub, getting what shade he could. By night he had walked north, taking his course by the Pole Star, and knowing that if he could only keep going he must eventually reach the coast road.

But of the pilot, Mackenzie, he could tell nothing, since the last he had seen of him was in the aircraft, only a minute or so before it crashed into the earth.

McConnell, the wireless operator-air gunner, was spotted from the air later in the same day, and his rescue only just came in time. He was crawling on hands and knees, too weak to walk. His chest appeared shrivelled to those who ran from the landed aircraft to pick him up. And he, like Fearn, was terribly disfigured by insect bites. He was so far gone in thirst that the doctor announced that he would have died in a few hours if he had not been picked up.

As in Fearn's case, he was quickly taken into the shade beneath the Bombay wing, allowed a very little water to drink, but doused with it all over his emaciated body. And those who were standing by saw a peculiar sight. As water was poured over him, it disappeared upon his blackened skin like drips on the top of a hot stove.

Happily, McConnell also survived, and in the course of time reached robust health again. But he could tell no more about Mackenzie than Fearn had already told.

The air search, with a big Valencia aircraft carrying military policemen with motor-cycles, was continued. The maximum distance that any man could have walked from the crashed aircraft was doubled, and plotted on a map. Since the crash had not burned, and since there were no bones of any kind among the wreckage, it was perfectly obvious that Mackenzie had not been in it when it went in. There was also the parachute found a mile away, and the supposed footprints . . . and the cut shroud lines.

For days on end the entire area in which he could have walked in any direction from the crash was combed by motor-cycle police and by low-flying aircraft. Nothing whatever was found.

From the first moment to the last of the search, no vultures were seen anywhere about. In that part of the desert there are no wild animals by which he could have been attacked either before or after his death. Moreover, so intensive was the search that all concerned reported themselves absolutely certain that had his skeleton been lying anywhere, they would have been sure to see it.

Only one credible explanation of the parachute and the cut cords has ever been offered. The supposed footprints which led to it from the crashed aircraft could indicate that Mackenzie—if it was he—might have been injured, and lamed. The broken stick suggested that he had used it as a splint which he then tied on with the cords from the parachute in order to support his injured leg. Whatever happened after that, one thing is quite certain. No man in his condition could have walked more than a mile or two from that point. But from there the vague prints in the desert faded out. They did not reappear anywhere. If Mackenzie had baled out after Fearn, landed and carried his parachute to the point where it was found, and then made his splint . . . where had he gone?

Only one person in the world could ever answer that question, and that was Flying Officer Mackenzie, a very gallant airman.

5

HANGED BY THE NECK

In September 1940, when the Battle of Britain was at its height, Sergeant Pilot F. S. Perkin was a member of the famous 73 Squadron based on Castle Camps, Essex. At that time this satellite of Debden aerodrome was nothing much more than a few fields thrown into one, with a bunch of Nissen huts and a marquee for general accommodation.

Perkin had, up to this time, done two operational trips in the Hurricane single-seater fighter aircraft with which '73'—and most of the other fighter squadrons of the Royal Air Force—were then equipped. Although the famous Spitfires had already come into service, the bulk of the battle was fought in Hurricanes which, although more manœuvrable than the enemy's Me109s, could not match them in speed. However, history showed that this little point had no more effect on the pilots of Fighter Command than the mighty Armada had on Drake's lads a few hundred years beforehand.

Meanwhile, Sergeant Perkin was feeling somewhat relaxed and luxurious, since the Squadron had not been ordered to be at 'readiness' until 9 am. For the first time after many days of having to scramble out before dawn, Perkin and his friends lay slothfully in bed until 7.30, and thereafter took their time over dressing and breakfast. Then they lounged about in their hut listening to a 'bind' on the forthcoming day's work, the formation to be adopted, and kindred matters. While this was in progress the telephone rang and the man nearest to it, having listened for a moment, slammed it back on its rest.

'Scramble—Thames Estuary—Angels 20,' he said briefly.

But almost before he had finished speaking, the hut was filled with plunging bodies, as men grabbed for their gloves, helmets and gear, and went streaming out of the door and across the airfield.

In ordinary English, their telephone orders were to get off the ground forthwith and climb to a height of 20000 feet over the estuary of the River Thames, there to take on any enemy aircraft which might appear, or to act under further radio orders from the Control Room.

Sergeant Perkin, getting a move on with the rest, was annoyed to find that someone had swiped his gloves. He bellowed at a rigger to get him another pair as he clambered up into the cockpit of his aircraft and started buckling up and plugging in his gear. By the time the man got back to hand up a pair of gloves, Perkin was fuming with impatience because he could already see the leading aircraft trundling off to start their take-off run. He wrenched his gloves on and reached up for his canopy to slam it shut, but the rigger, outside, held it back.

'Better do your leg straps up, Sarge,' he said.

Perkin glanced down at his own lap and saw that in his impatience he had forgotten to fasten the all-important leg straps of his parachute to the centre harness buckle. If the rigger had not noticed it, the end of this story would have been different; tragically so. Perkin nodded his thanks as he attached the straps. It was the first—and the last—time in his flying career that he ever made such a mistake.

A few minutes later he was away off the ground, feeling the satisfying clicks as his undercarriage wheels retracted and locked. He climbed to catch up with the rest of the Squadron, finally taking up his place just behind the right wing of his Squadron Leader as they orbited over base. Behind him were the rest of the chaps of '73', many of whose names became famous in Fighter Command as the war went on; 'One-arm Mac' Maclachlan, who later in the war had a claw at the end of a steel mechanism with which he worked the engine controls in place of his missing right arm, and did his shooting with his left hand; the big, cheerful, stuttering Jas Storrar; the handsome and witty Mike Beytagh, who was afterwards to fight through the desert campaign and command the City of Glasgow Squadron in the closing stages of the war, to name only a few. In tight formation the Squadron climbed to 20000 feet above the river estuary in the bright sunshine of mid-morning. Then the controller's voice came over the radio: 'Twenty escorted bandits approaching Burnham.'

The Squadron turned obediently, but before they had Burnham beneath them, radioed orders came through again: 'Fifty Ju88s approaching Clacton at Angels 5.'

Unnecessary natter (talk) over the R/T was officially discouraged, but there were those who offered an opinion about the controller as the Squadron Leader altered course again and led his followers in a dive to 5000 feet. As they went, everyone strained their eyes ahead and around, but there was nothing to be seen in the vast blue bowl of the sunlit sky.

Clacton appeared unmistakably on the coastline far below . . . at which point the controller suddenly came through and ordered them back to 20000 feet where a large force of enemy fighters were reported to be milling around.

Perkin was amused to hear Jas Storrar's famous stutter: 'O—oh, bub-bub-*blast*!' but he immediately opened up again and started the long climb back into the heights, steadily in his place on the Squadron Leader's right wing. Nothing could be seen in the brilliant glare of the sun.

Still the formation was kept very tight, flying in three vics of three aircraft each with two 'weaving' in the rear. These two swung from side to side as they flew, so that they could get a wider range of view all round and would be able to spot unexpected attack and warn their comrades ahead.

At least that was the general idea at the time. Different tactics were adopted later on, especially in conditions of brilliant sunlight. It was this factor which beat the weavers on this occasion. Neither they nor any other pilot in the Squadron caught a glimpse of the enemy attack which was even then coming down at them out of the blinding glare of the sun.

At that moment Perkin had his eye on the coastline below. He had just checked height at around 22000 feet on the altimeter, and was marking the town of Colchester. Then he was startled by what seemed to be an explosion in his Merlin engine immediately in front of him. In actual fact that 'explosion' was the impact of a burst of cannon shells from an enemy fighter which had dived directly upon him from out of the sun. In the next moment Perkin's cockpit was filled with flames. The enemy cannon shell had hit his reserve tank and the petrol had 'gone up'.

The attack was so sudden and unexpected that he had had no chance of either taking evasive action or fighting back. At one moment he was checking position; at the next his cockpit was on fire and he could feel the flames at work on the skin of his hands and face. There was only one thing he could do—get out, fast.

Perkin reached up, slammed his canopy back and jerked out the hart pin which secured his Sutton harness. With the straps sliding over his shoulders he heaved up to get himself out of the blast of the fire, and over the side of the aircraft. But something stuck. What it was he had no idea at the time. He pushed, and kicked his legs to free them of whatever had got tangled. When at last he got clear and went over the side, he had the unpleasant impression that he had managed to kick his parachute off as well in the general upheaval.

When he told me the story afterwards, Perkin's own words were the usual fighter-pilot understatement.

"Something seems to happen to your mind at a moment like that," he said quietly. "I know I didn't care whether I'd got a parachute on or not. I only wanted to get away from the damned fire."

Perkin got away, but only by a matter of feet. He had no sooner tumbled over the side than he was pulled up with a tremendous jerk which seemed as though it had dislocated his neck. In his scramble to get himself out of the fire he had not had time to undo his oxygen and R/T leads, the ends of which were firmly plugged inside the burning cockpit, while the other ends were still connected to the helmet which was strapped round his head.

For the next few seconds Perkin hung by his helmet, anchored to the burning Hurricane, which went diving down the sky in an uncontrolled spin, leaving a whirling trail of flame and smoke behind it. He was completely helpless. At the speed at which he was being dragged he could not get his hands up with enough strength to unbuckle the helmet strap.

Fortunately, however, the helmet had not been designed to withstand strains of that order. The strap suddenly broke, and then Sergeant Perkin performed a spirited somersault head over heels over the burning aircraft's tail . . . which he felt was hardly a text-book departure.

As he went down the sky, still turning head over heels, his first clear sensation was that of deep relief in the cool draught against the skin of his face and hands. When the daze of his neck-wrenching wore off he realized that he had better find out if his parachute had really been kicked off. With some relief he found that it hadn't. He grabbed the release ring, gave it a hearty wrench and found that the handle came away in his hand trailing about a yard of cord.

This seemed to indicate that his parachute pack had either been shot away or burnt to uselessness by the fire. Perkin tensed himself to face one of the more unpleasant methods of departing this life. Then he heard a thudding crack from above, felt a violent jerk on his body harness, and glanced up to see the white parachute canopy fully opened above with its shroud lines supporting him with comforting strength.

When he discovered that providence had given him at least an extension of life, Perkin allowed himself to relax and look around. He found he wasn't alone. A Hurricane was making steep turns all around his parachute, and he recognized Scotty, a comrade. Scotty's occupation became obvious as Perkin again grew conscious of the roar and drone of aircraft close at hand. He looked up to see the sky above still filled with Hurricanes and Me109s diving and climbing and rolling all around in a general uproar of open exhausts and thudding armaments. Scotty meanwhile was playing guard to his helpless comrade, circling round the drifting parachute ready to discourage German pilots from their light-hearted habit of shooting down men who had had to bale out.

Perkin waved his thanks for the protection offered. Then he felt a bit queer and, as he hung in his parachute harness, he was suddenly and shatteringly sick. In the moments of giddy nausea that followed he became sharply conscious of the smell of burnt flying-suit and skin, which hung about him like an aura. By the time he recovered himself, he found he was in an empty sky and that the uproar of exhausts and machine guns had died away. This sudden change will not surprise any who have had experience of aerial combat. The effect of the speed of even the piston-engined aircraft of the Second World War was such that the sky could be full of a howling dog fight one minute, and apparently clear at the next.

Perkin, however, realized that he now had only a few hundred feet of height left and that he was coming down squarely in the middle of the Thames Estuary, with about five or six miles of water stretching on either side of him to the shores of Kent or Essex. There was no shipping of any kind in sight and the prospect looked distinctly unpleasant until he saw that there was a strip of sandbank not far away. He marked its position carefully as he drifted down. Then the shining surface of the water seemed to make a sudden rush upwards—and with a heavy splash he was in it.

He remembered his parachute drill clearly enough. He clapped undone the harness release as soon as he struck the surface. He was clear of it when he came up again and to his relief still had the sandbank in sight. But as he struck out and started swimming towards it his mind was occupied with thoughts about quicksands . . .

When at last his feet touched bottom and he staggered forward, still breast high in the water, he found to his relief that the sand was firm. Soon he had managed to wade out on the shallow top of the bank and then once again he heard a Merlin engine. Looking up he saw the faithful Scotty circling around him again, flying at only about 10 feet of height as slowly as possible with wheels and flaps down. Once again Perkin waved, this time to show that he was alive with no bones broken, and the reassured Scotty forthwith opened up and flew off shorewards to give his position and organize rescue.

For the next twenty minutes Perkin sat on his sandbank and hoped that what he had heard of the curative qualities of salt water as applied to burns was true. During that time he saw another parachute drift down on to the Isle of Sheppey, and afterwards learned that it was his comrade Jim Lang. Meanwhile, however, he had actually been spotted from the shore and, before the rescue organized by Scotty had time to get to him, a couple of fishermen came rowing up in a boat to take him on board.

. . . . .

When I checked the details of Perkin's story with him and told him that I wanted to include it in these pages, his reaction was very typical of the RAF.

"Well, frankly," he said, "I can't help feeling that the idea is a bit nauseating. My experience is not specially different from dozens of others. I've talked to you about it because you asked me—because you are another RAF chap. But I don't like the idea of any blood and thunder getting into print."

It took considerable explanation and reasoning to get his permission, which only came grudgingly after I had promised that there would be no blood and thunder, only a factual report on almost the same lines he had had to give at his own de-briefing. Also, that other men for whom he had all respect and admiration had given their stories on the same assurance.

And when finally, to turn the conversation, I asked him what he felt about the whole incident now that he could look back on it after a period of thirteen years, his reply was just as typical. It dealt with nothing concerning himself or his feelings.

"My dear chap," he said, "the thing I feel most about it is the way we just asked for trouble in those days. We flew such clottishly close formation—nearly everyone was watching everyone else instead of keeping their eyes open all around them. Before we learned to fly a more open formation we were just *bound* to get jumped by the Hun in the sun."

6

BRADLEY TRIES A BUNT

ONE of the truest of Royal Air Force axioms holds that 'there are bold pilots, there are old pilots, but there are very few old bold pilots'. All who have much experience of flying, either in the Service or otherwise, have learnt the grim truth of this. Most of us can remember moments during our over-confident earlier days when fate suddenly seemed to make all our chances of living to a ripe old age very remote.

Flight Cadet Jack Bradley found his special moment of this kind while he was at the Royal Air Force College, Cranwell. One fine afternoon he was detailed to take a Siskin III fighter on a height test, and as a dutiful young budding officer he proceeded to carry out orders forthwith.

Now, if you have ever had to deal with pilots during their training you will very soon discover that the most difficult part of the job is to preserve a young chap's natural fighting spirit. This may sound easy, but his fighting spirit is part of his natural instinct to break rules, fool about, and try to prove to himself that he isn't frightened by attempting most of the dangerous things he has been forbidden to try. The result is that he very often ends his career, and that of a valuable aircraft, suddenly and dismally in a cloud of black smoke. In terms of hard cash his training up to that point has usually been almost as expensive to the taxpayer as the machine he wrecks. There is also the fact that he is a cheerful character and well liked both by his instructors and his comrades.

The true fighting spirit beneath the damn foolishness is a very valuable side of our young friend's character. Those who train him try to preserve it. They curse him with artistic fervour; they call down disciplinary thunders upon his errant head; they think up penalties for fat-headed procedure in the air which will make him squirm . . . and all the time they hope to God that they can keep him alive without spoiling his fighting spirit, until he has gained the real experience that will enable him (sometimes) to make rude signs in the face of Providence, and get away with it.

In this respect, Flight Cadet Jack Bradley was neither better nor worse than the average young man whose one object in life is to fly a fighter aircraft. He was a naturally good pilot, and if he took chances it was because he was genuinely interested in flying, and in getting the best out of his machine, than in trying to impress himself or anybody else. After having carried out his height test, therefore, and when he was at about 16000 feet, Bradley decided to liven the proceedings by doing a 'bunt'.

This is an evolution which has for years been regarded with the dimmest possible of views by Their Lordships of the Air Council, as well as by all pilots who have reached years of aerial discretion. The 'bunt' is the reverse of a loop. When a pilot loops he first dives his aircraft and gets up a good speed, and then climbs sharply, going over on his back and then diving down again to complete the full circle. His head, it will be understood, is on the *inside* of this circle all the time, and his body is so firmly pushed into the aircraft by centrifugal force that he cannot possibly fall out, even at the point where he is upside-down.

In the 'bunt' he does things precisely the other way round. Having started his dive, he dives steeper and still steeper—and faster and still faster—pushing his control forward until the aircraft has dived itself upside-down and is beginning to climb up the other way. If he can make it climb up to the top of the circle he is right way up again. But all the time his head has been on the *outside* of the circle and centrifugal force has been trying to fling him out of the aeroplane. Throughout the whole of the evolution he is hanging in his safety harness with his blood being flung up towards his head.

Quite apart from its effects on the pilot, a bunt imposes tremendous strains on the aircraft itself, and has for years been on the list of things forbidden. Incidentally, at the speeds of modern aircraft—whether jet or piston—the evolution is totally impossible, anyway.

Flight Cadet Bradley found it impossible in the Siskin. Just what happened he didn't know, but when he got over the vertical in his dive—that is, upside-down—he found that the aircraft would not start climbing. In fact, he found no response to the elevator control or the actuating gear. Naturally, therefore, he cut his engine and attempted to roll; that is, to turn the aircraft right way up. At first nothing whatever happened, and the speed of his upside-down, head-long dive was increasing alarmingly.

At his second attempt he succeeded up to a point. He got the machine over so that his head was at least pointing in the right direction, but at the same time his dive was still steep and he reckoned he was proceeding at around 300 miles an hour.

To try to correct this he moved the wheel which actuated the tail incidence and wound it back, hoping to bring the nose of the aircraft up again.

It was at this moment that something made him glance aside out of his cockpit, which was just as well, for he was in time to see his two lower planes leave the machine and disappear behind him. This he found depressing, but worse was to come. When he glanced up, naturally enough, to see how the top planes were getting on, he saw with a shock that they had already departed. Then something hit him heavily across the face. He thought, vaguely, that it was a bit of cowling.

In the crazily detached way that affects men in moments of this kind he heard someone shout quite loudly : 'Good God' . . . and realized that it was himself.

Bradley's position at this stage of the proceedings was unenviable. He was diving down the sky at screaming speed in the wingless fuselage of a heavy fighter aircraft which had no visible means of support. Since such a machine was far from respectable, he decided to leave it forthwith. He therefore whipped the quick-release pin out of his safety harness, and, as the straps obediently flew off, unplugged all gear that connected him with the cockpit. He then found that he couldn't get out anyhow, for the wingless fuselage had now started to spin wildly as it dived earthwards. Centrifugal force was now playing him another trick. It pressed him so hard against the left side of the spinning cockpit that for a moment he couldn't move. It was a moment in which he reflected that a lot of things had been happening since first his wings fell off . . . and he didn't know how much height he had left in hand. Strong measures were indicated.

Bradley put out all his strength and gradually forced himself up, digging his elbows on to the cockpit edge. As he did so the remaining part of the aeroplane behaved just as aeroplanes usually do when you don't want any complications. He found his right foot caught by something, and held fast. He gave a raging kick and got it free, minus his right shoe. By now he knew that he couldn't beat the force which held him into the wildly spinning machine with his own muscles. In fact he realized he would not be able to jump clear. Therefore he got one hand free, groped for his parachute ring and yanked it hard.

The danger of releasing a parachute whilst one is still in an aircraft will be obvious. All the chances are in favour of the life-saving silken envelope catching in a tailplane and remaining anchored, or ripping itself to pieces on some other part of the machine. Even so, the parachute was the one chance Bradley had left of getting out of the spinning wreck, and although the odds against him were around several hundreds to one, he took the bet.

Next moment he had the unpleasant sight of the pilot-chute bellying out between his legs, and then winding itself round his left leg just below the knee. The pilot-chute is the small one which helps to pull out the larger one and inflate it.

For an instant he thought this was the end, but the luck which had been having such freakish fun with him suddenly decided to turn friendly. Something made him glance down under the crook of his left arm and there, to his vast relief, he saw the main parachute ripping and streaming out in the ferocious draught. Then, to quote his own words, 'there was a colossal crack, and something suddenly grabbed me and whipped me out of the fuselage.'

His parachute opened, but owing to the tremendous speed its force of pulling him clear of his harness knocked him breathless. Later on he found one small matter that gave evidence of that sudden strain. His front collar-stud had been broken clean in half.

As he began swinging gently under the parachute, which to his amazement showed a surface of untorn fabric, Bradley admits that he thanked God for a very considerable mercy. Then he had the idea that he drifted into fog, but realized that his goggles had misted over—there being understandable reason on his part for perspiration—so he pushed them up on to his forehead. At once he felt blood streaming down across his face. Although he dabbed gingerly with his hands and felt about, he could not locate the injury, but discovered afterwards that his lips had been badly torn.

He heard the sound of an engine and looked about

him to see an Atlas aircraft circling round close by. Since Bradley knew that the remains of his wings must be coming down somewhere in the vicinity, he waved violently to the Atlas pilot and gestured to him to get clear. Then, hanging on to his harness webs, he craned his neck for a look upwards, and saw one of his wings floating down just beyond the edge of his parachute envelope, and about 300 feet above. A few seconds later he saw another which was wafting and spinning even higher. He realized that they were falling faster than he was, now that he was floating on his parachute, and one of them looked as if it was going to come straight down on to him canopy, and either collapse it or tear it in half.

Since this was Bradley's first jump, he was naturally no parachute expert. But he started to do everything he had read or heard about by way of side-slipping out of the way of the falling wing. He pulled with all his strength on the left-hand parachute cords, but he seemed to be just lifting his own body up without causing the canopy to veer in its path in any way. He tried again fiercely, since the wings threatened him with just as unpleasant a form of death as that from which he had been saved, but still he got no joy. Whether or not he actually managed to move the parachute in its path he never afterwards knew, but to his immense relief he suddenly saw the wings coming down and passing him, close on either hand, one spinning slowly and the other gliding in a succession of 'falling-leaf' motions. But the fact that they were only descending a little faster than he was brought an unpleasant thought to his mind.

A falling wing, he reasoned, must go down pretty fast and the wings were not passing him quickly. Therefore he must be falling rather fast himself, much too fast for a comfortable landing. He remembered now that the 'back'-type parachute-pack used in the Siskins was smaller than the normal type. He knew his weight to be well over twelve stone and, by reason of the height test he had been ordered to carry out, he was wearing a heavy Sidcot suit. The present prospect, therefore, was not pleasing, especially when he realized that all small details of the ground were swiftly becoming very much clearer. He had an idea that he ought to equalize the force of his landing, and therefore kicked off his one remaining shoe. A coppice of trees was sweeping up towards him, so he fiercely tried hauling on the shrouds of the parachute to attempt a side-slip again. Since the wings had missed him, he thought he must have succeeded the first time without clearly realizing it. As the wood suddenly changed direction beneath him, he saw that his idea had been true enough. It is not easy for a 'first tripper' to gauge whether or not he is side-slipping his parachute when he is high above the ground.

The speed of his second side-slip was brisk, and as the trees and the ground whipped past beneath his feet he saw that he was travelling backwards in the grip of a strong wind. That, as far as he had ever heard, was just about the most dangerous way to land from any parachute, so he tried to turn round. In an effort to turn he pulled down on one of the four main supports—and then, as nothing happened, on the diagonal ones. Still the parachute refused to start turning. He yanked on the two at one side and the two at the back . . . but only started penduluming sickeningly. By now he realized he was moving over fields of small crops, but as he worked frantically he reckoned he was probably going to be dead within a minute or two.

He hit the ground just when he least expected it—as is usually the way with first jumpers—rolled head over heels, collapsed, and then scrambled on to his knees, quite unhurt and astounded that his landing hadn't broken most of the bones in his body.

As Flight Cadet Bradley stood in the middle of that small cornfield and wrenched his harness free, he breathed deeply and thought about the ways of Providence. Then, as he began to gather in the life-saving silken folds of his parachute, he thought about his forthcoming interview with his Squadron Commander.

7

GREAT HEART

THIS is the story of one of the finest Victoria Crosses won in the Second World War. In the course of this action five men qualified for the badge of the Caterpillar Club. Those others died.

Towards the latter end of 1942, RAF Bomber Command was giving a good deal of attention to Northern Italy. There were two reasons for this. The first was to keep the enemy Air Force well occupied, and so reduce its ability to harass the Allied landings in North Africa. It was also thought possible at the time—and proved to be a fact, later—that heavy bombing of Italy, added to the Allied victories in North Africa, would seriously undermine the morale of the Italian people.

That this worked is a matter of history. Italy, as everyone knows, became more of a liability than a help to the German war effort, and finally collapsed as a fighting nation, going clean out of the war. The fact that Bomber Command of the Royal Air Force had a great deal to do with this has been underlined in the official histories.

The offensive began with the raid on Genoa by a force of 112 bombers on the night of October 22nd and was followed by twelve major attacks during the next two months, the main force of the attacks being directed at that port and the big manufacturing cities of Milan and Turin. The first raid on Milan caused a wild panic, and a large number of the inhabitants departed from the city and did not return again.

For the aircrews of Bomber Command, however, these long-distance raids were a tremendous test of guts, endurance, skill in navigation and all that goes to make up the business of airmanship. Apart from the distance, there was the great barrier of the Alps over which the aircraft had to fly both on the outward and home journeys. As is natural in the Air Force, the boys who were doing the job said nothing about their difficulties except amongst themselves, since grousing is one of the most precious privileges of the Service. Their only remarks which became public had to do with the excellent visibility they usually found over the Italian cities, and the lighter concentration of flak that met them when they got there.

Said one of them to me: "Well, it's a hell of a long whiz, sir, and it's nice when you've dropped your load and can turn for home. But, apart from the mountains, it's a piece of cake. You can get down to nought feet. You can really get smack on your targets. They chuck up a certain amount of stuff at you, but it's nowhere so bad as the Ruhr."

The towering mountain range of the Alps was the bogey which affected them all. On the night of November 29th the freezing cold and contrary winds over the Alpine range played havoc with the force which had been detailed to Turin. Only half of them got to the target. One of the pilots who returned had this to say afterwards about the 'show'.

'As we flew over the Alps, rain and low cloud brought the visibility down to a matter of a few yards. It was already bitterly cold, but as we began climbing up to cross the mountains the icing became fierce. We started to get a whole lot of fun-and-games from electrical storms. The whole thing was a bit dicey. I saw ice flying off the wing in large chunks and heard it clattering back against the fuselage . . .'

Half this force had to turn back with fuel shortage,

icing trouble and other difficulties, some getting almost there before having to turn back. Amongst the aircraft which actually did reach the target and deliver its bomb load was one piloted by Sergeant R. H. Middleton of the Royal Australian Air Force, who had a crew of seven with him in his Stirling aircraft.

Flight Sergeant L. A. Hyder was second pilot. Navigator, Pilot Officer G. R. Royde; wireless operator, Pilot Officer Norman Skinner; flight engineer, Sergeant J. E. Jeffery; front-gunner, Sergeant Mackie; mid-upper gunner, Flight Sergeant D. Cameron; and rear-gunner, Sergeant H. W. Gough. The quality of this crew is shown by the fact that the last three men named had actually finished their tour of operations. Nevertheless, they wanted to stay with Middleton, their captain, and after some argument were given permission to go along with him on the raid.

While the aircraft was droning across the countryside of France, Middleton realized that she was not climbing as well as she should. He knew he would need 14000 feet of clear height in order to get over the Alps, and asked for a report from Jeffery, the engineer.

"If we go on at this rate, Skipper, we haven't got enough juice to get us back to base," reported Jeffery. "It's taken us a hell of a time to get to 12000 feet and we've still got to climb. With any luck we may get back as far as the English coast, but it'll be chancy."

Middleton looked at the weather, which was already bad. He weighed things in his mind but then gave his decision. "We'll carry on," he said, and it was typical of his crew that not one word of dissension came from any of them. Even so, as the aircraft approached the Alpine area, refusing to climb any higher, Middleton saw that his altimeter still showed only 12000 feet—2000 feet less than the safety limit for the mountain crossing.

He spoke to Royde, the navigator.

"See if you can pick us out a pass," he requested

cheerfully. "I can't get the old girl up far enough to clear the tops, but if we can find a good pass, we can scrape through."

Without a word of protest Royde got busy with his maps. Soon the vast crags and pinnacles of the mountains were looming dead ahead—and above—the approaching aircraft, a barrier of snow and ice towering into the darkness in which no moon was showing. Middleton did not hesitate. He steered the heavily-laden aircraft on Royde's course, which led into a slight depression between two peaks. A few seconds later they were flying along a perilously narrow defile with snow-covered peaks towering above them on either side.

"Keep your eyes skinned, everybody," ordered Middleton calmly. "We'll be all right coming back. We'll have dropped our load so that we can climb. But help keep a look-out now."

His crew did so with more than dutiful concentration. The defile between the towering peaks of the mountains twisted and turned, and Middleton banked and swung the big aircraft round each curve with the skill of a trick cyclist. At times it seemed that the wing-tips only missed the rock face on either side by a matter of feet. Then Cameron, the mid-upper gunner, suddenly let out a yell.

"Peak ahead, Skipper," he bellowed. "Watch out. Dead ahead."

Middleton, fortunately, saw it almost at the same time. For an instant all on board had the terrible conviction that they were flying straight into a vast, snow-covered wall of rock. But then, just as quickly, the way past it flashed into view. Middleton took the aircraft round without the slightest show of uncertainty or nerves.

Gough, the rear-gunner, gulped slightly as he saw the rock wall whip past his draughty position at what seemed rather like inches. When he had steadied himself he spoke into the intercom.

"By Christ, chum," he said to Cameron in the mid-upper turret, "I hope you see the next one before I do."

Worse was to come. The narrow pass began to close in beneath them. They realized that the bottom was becoming shallower, coming up and up, and it did not seem possible that the aircraft could scrape over it as it flattened out ahead, apparently higher than they were flying.

Middleton decided then that the attempt was impossible. Since there was no chance of striking at the enemy, his first duty was to save his crew. He decided to jettison the bomb load, and so get over the barrier with a lightened aircraft.

Just as he was about to give the order he realized that he was practically through the mountains. There were no more peaks, but far ahead in a clear valley he could actually see the city of Turin, brilliantly lit by flares dropped by aircraft which had already got there, and sparkling and blazing with the bombs which were being rained down. The sight made him hesitate about his order. Then he realized that he was too late. There was no time now to jettison the bombs; his aircraft was already thundering over the last of the high ground which was racing past, a matter of feet below the fuselage.

A second later they were actually out in the clear. They had got through. The pass and the Alps were left behind, and the already blazing target was in front. Middleton put the nose of the Stirling down and calmly began to discuss the run-up to their special objective, the Fiat works, with Hyder, the second-pilot, and the navigator, Royde. A lot of flak began to come up from the ground, but the flares were now diminishing and giving a view that was less clear. It was no easy matter to pick out the target for which they were making.

Middleton therefore took the aircraft down low and went looking for it, in spite of violent anti-aircraft fire. This was not as intense as the crew had met in other parts of Europe, but it was bad enough. Shells thudded and flashed around them as they picked up the position of the Fiat works and then made their first run-in. Middleton was not satisfied with this run or with the second. He banked the big aircraft round and came in for a third time, keeping dead steady on course so that the bombs could be accurately sent upon their way.

During these three runs the aircraft was repeatedly hit with light flak; the fuselage seemed filled with the stink of cordite fumes; and every man on board was thinking of the petrol tanks and the inevitable, final blaze if they received a direct hit.

Almost as soon as the bombs were away, the ground gunners seemed to get the range dead-on. Flak smashed through the mainplane and into the fuselage. The aircraft lurched over, and Middleton shouted to Hyder to help him hold it.

Hyder obeyed instinctively, although he had been badly wounded and was still half-dazed. As he did so, he was horrified to see that Middleton's right eye appeared to have been shot clean out, and the bone of his forehead was showing in an ugly red gash. Somehow, the two of them steadied the aircraft, flew it out of the concentration of fire and got on to course for the journey home, with the mountains once again ahead.

With his remaining good eye Middleton saw that Hyder had been badly hit.

"Get back to the fuselage and get yourself attended to," he ordered in a strained voice. "They've got some first-aid stuff back there."

Hyder protested but, since orders are orders, he was about to obey when he realized that Middleton had lost consciousness and collapsed over his controls. As a result, the aircraft went into a headlong dive which Hyder, wrenching fiercely at the column, was only able to pull out of at about 800 feet. Hyder stayed in control and began the climb back towards the Alps. As he did so, he called for a report from the crew.

Skinner, the wireless operator, announced that he was wounded in the leg, but could carry on. Gough, at the rear, reported that he was all right and had been returning fire at the ground the whole time until a burst hit his turret, twisting one of his guns almost at right angles and putting the hydraulic gear out of commission. Actually, he had been severely wounded in the process.

"Okay, chaps," said Hyder, privately wondering how long he could hang on to consciousness himself. "Get rid of all you can. Chuck everything movable over the side. We've got to get back over these mountains."

It was at this point that Middleton came to. Hyder believes that he was badly wounded in the stomach and in his right arm and leg in addition to his lost eye. Yet, as his senses cleared, he insisted on taking over control again while Hyder's wounds were attended to, as well as could be managed, by one of the others.

From that moment, throughout the long hours of the rest of the flight, Middleton remained at the controls and refused to hand over. With the bomb load gone and everything, including the guns, jettisoned, the Stirling climbed steadily and was soon well above 14000 feet and flying back over the Alps again, well above the topmost peaks. By now the moon had come out, but although it provided a really lovely spectacle, it was by no means welcomed by the crew. They had still the long run across France to cover.

The question of fuel was now uppermost in everybody's mind. Fortunately, as far as they knew, the tanks had not been hit and the engines were running steadily. But Engineer Jeffery reported that even with the wind, which had now swung round and was in their favour, they could not hope to scrape back further than the English coast at best.

The badly-wounded Middleton again had to consider things carefully. On the fuel they had they could be sure of reaching dry land either in North Africa or in

Switzerland. By going straight ahead they risked death from enemy-fighter attack—or a ditching in the North Sea, somewhere short of the coast, if they were still alive when they got there.

"I'm going straight on, chaps," said Middleton. "I'm going to try for home. With this wind we ought to be able to make the coast. Have a look round and see that there isn't anything left to go overboard."

Once again, none of the crew offered any question as to his decision. With the Alps behind them and the engines running regularly, their hopes began to rise as they crossed over the vast plain of France. Then, suddenly, a searchlight swung up from the ground and caught them. Another flicked on; another; and yet another. Soon an octopus of white fingers was reaching up into the sky and feeling for them.

Middleton's endurance seemed miraculous to Hyder. He threw the Stirling into a weaving path of evasion. It was a wildly hectic period which none who survived it will ever forget. How Middleton managed it they never knew. Quite apart from anything else, the front windscreen of the aircraft had been blown out when the flak first hit, and from that time right through the freezing heights above the Alps he had been sitting in an icy gale.

At last they realized that by his skill they were out of immediate danger. He dodged the searchlights which had threatened them. He weaved and turned and finally drew out of their range, so that, after aimless groping about the sky in the rear, one after another of them snapped out.

Then came the tremendous moment when at last the Stirling crew saw the silver glitter of the sea ahead. As they flew out over it, Middleton called for his last fuel report from Jeffery.

"Five minutes, Skipper," answered Jeffery. "Maybe ten with blind luck, but I shouldn't think so."

Middleton held the aircraft on course flying straight

on above the Channel. When he spoke again, his voice was noticeably weak.

"Prepare to bale out, everybody," he ordered, "and one of you bring me my parachute pack."

The last part of that order, Hyder believes, Middleton gave purely in order to reassure them all. He must have known in those last moments that he had become far too weak to get himself out of his seat. All he was thinking about was their safety. Meanwhile, he still kept control, occasionally swaying in his seat, but Hyder could see that he was staying conscious. The English coast appeared like a shadow ahead, gradually drew nearer, and was at last directly beneath them. But still Middleton kept on. He flew straight inland for a distance of about two miles, then he spoke the last words that any living man heard from him.

"All right," said Middleton. "Jump, everybody."

As a matter of record, at that moment he had been eight solid hours in his pilot's seat. For four and a half of those hours he had been severely and painfully wounded in the body and had lost one eye. Throughout the whole of that epic flight he had kept full control of the machine except for a few moments of unconsciousness after he had first been hit.

When the order to bale out finally came, Mackie, the front-gunner, saw that Hyder was too weak to move. He therefore hauled him to the escape hatch, thrust the release handle of his parachute into his hand, and then shoved him bodily out. Royde, Cameron and Gough went next, followed by the badly wounded Skinner. Jeffery and Mackie were still on board with Middleton as the aircraft roared away above the parachutes that were opening and drifting down in the darkness.

The bodies of Jeffery and Mackie were washed ashore next day, but of the aircraft nothing was ever seen again. Skinner, the last man to go, knew that Middleton had already turned it towards the sea. More than probably

Middleton knew that in his fainting condition he would never be able to crash-land without endangering the lives of villagers or townsfolk. He must have been in intense pain, and it is fairly certain that with the reaction of losing one eye, the sight of the remaining one was badly affected. Therefore he evidently decided to make for the sea even though he knew that should he 'ditch' successfully the chances of his being rescued before the aircraft sank were absolutely nil.

Some time later Middleton's body was also recovered. Now it lies in a country churchyard beneath a small white cross which carries the inscription :

Flight Sergeant R. H. Middleton, VC,
Royal Australian Air Force.

At the burial service the chaplain recited over the body of this magnificently courageous young man, who had left a sheep farm in Leewing, Australia, to fight for an ideal of decency, the beautiful phrase :

'Thou knowest, Lord, the secrets of our hearts.'

8

CATERPILLAR GROUNDLING

SERGEANT McCANDLISH suffered from an enquiring mind. He also suffered from air sickness, yet he was fond of flying (a parodox which is often to be found amongst the 'ground types' in the Royal Air Force).

It may be as well to point out here that the dashing chaps in Air Force blue who wear winged badges on their chests couldn't do any dashing about the sky at all if it were not for their wingless brethren. Those undistinguished, hard-working and courageous brethren went to the ends of the earth throughout the war to keep the aeroplanes of their flying comrades in serviceable condition . . . and got malaria and dysentery and sunstroke, and starved and thirsted, and were taken prisoner by (and escaped from) Italian, German and Japanese hands . . . and died just as finely when it came to the point, or managed to blaspheme their way, still living, to final victory and peace.

In November 1943, Sergeant McCandlish and a number of other ground types serviced the aircraft of 45 Squadron in Assam. Sometimes they wondered why the Japanese forces were so keen to occupy what they regarded as a highly undesirable and altogether inhospitable area of the earth's surface. Still, the orders were that the Japanese must be encouraged to leave, and so the ground types and air types of 45 Squadron dutifully provided that encouragement to the best of their ability. At that time, however, the Japanese troops were not in a mood to take a hint—and replied with all known forms of lethal counter-attack, including intensive bombing of 45 Squadron's airstrip. They also had a habit of treating any captives who fell into their hands with a certain Oriental ingenuity which even the German mind at its most inspired has seldom matched.

It was therefore considered unwise to fall into Japanese hands by all concerned with '45'. Naturally enough, the flying members of the Squadron were in far greater danger of doing so than the others. Nevertheless, Sergeant McCandlish volunteered to go flying.

This is where we get back to his inquiring mind. As duty signals NCO, McCandlish had been bothered and puzzled by a certain piece of radio equipment which was a standard fitting. In this equipment a detonator was set to blow the whole thing up if it was subjected to a very heavy shock, such as would result from the aircraft crashing. The object, of course, was to prevent it from getting into enemy hands intact, so that it might be copied.

This was well enough in theory, but in practice McCandlish had recently found that the detonators had for some reason been blowing up and wrecking the apparatus whilst the aircraft was in flight—in fact, while it was receiving no heavy shock at all. The explosion, it will be understood, was not violent enough to damage any machine or do more than startle a wireless operator-air gunner almost out of his pants. Nevertheless, apparatus was getting wrecked unnecessarily, and in this far-flung corner of the war there wasn't any spare apparatus going begging.

McCandlish considered the matter, sat down and drew the sort of incomprehensible little drawings beloved of wireless enthusiasts. He then went to his Flight Commander and asked permission to test out a theory in the air. The Flight Commander frowned his indecision. He had the seasoned officer's natural distrust of experts; he also had to be sure that his serviceable aircraft should remain so for a special job the next day. Already that morning the Japs had bombed the airfield pretty smartly and he didn't want further trouble.

McCandlish saw the indecision and urged his point. His main idea was to take a test instrument with him in a rear cockpit and check certain results.

"All I want, sir, is for the pilot to do an operational dive with the bomb doors open," said the groundling. "There must be some reason for these detonations, sir. I want to simulate as nearly as possible conditions which might cause them. I reckon, if only I can make a proper test . . ."

The Flight Commander sighed and then grinned.

"OK," he said. "Get your gubbinses together and draw yourself a parachute. Mathews can take you, but if he breaks the aircraft or you gum it up in any way, I'll scrag you both. In any case, you're a damn nuisance. It'll mean an extra inspection of the kite before it takes off tomorrow. But your own little friends will probably give you their views about that. All right, hook it, and get teed up."

Dutifully, Sergeant McCandlish hooked it. He repaired within the wire entanglement which he was pleased to call a workshop, selected certain instruments and then called in at the parachute store, drawing himself a regulation pack. Then he sought out a mess companion, Flight Sergeant Mathews, and smiled upon him.

"For Pete's sake," protested Mathews wearily, "what's this trip you've wished upon me?"

McCandlish explained about detonating charges in the sort of words he hoped would appeal to a non-scientific mind.

"Oh-ah," said Flight Sergeant Mathews. "Well, if it doesn't take too long I suppose it's all right. Anyway, the CO says I've got to take you. But no playing about . . ."

Sergeant McCandlish agreed that he would not play about. He also emphasized that the various dives he wanted the aircraft to carry out should be with the bomb doors open, adding that he thought it might be in the interests of safety all round if the dives were not carried out in the immediate vicinity of their home airstrip, having regard to the fact that the home ack-ack gunners were inclined to be a bit trigger-happy.

With this Flight Sergeant Mathews concurred as he led the way to the aircraft and climbed up into his seat. Immediately an attendant flight crew appeared to give both airmen help and attention.

Said one, addressing McCandlish cheerfully, "Well, I hope you know how to bale out, Mac."

Said Flight Sergeant Mathews from the front seat, in a tone of mordant humour, "All I hope is that Mac knows how to operate the wireless."

Sergeant McCandlish disregarded this cheerful insult to his own trade and busied himself with all those fiddlings and connections which drive practitioners of other professions to a state of profanity.

A few minutes later the engine was roaring and they were away. When they were climbing comfortably, and the occupant of the front cockpit was satisfied with the readings of his various dials, he asked a question over the intercom.

"You there, Mac?" he inquired. "Are you feeling all right?"

Part of his concern was because he happened to like Sergeant McCandlish. The other part was due to the fact that he knew McCandlish's failing of air sickness . . . and, like many another pilot, he was sensitive about the condition of his aircraft. McCandlish, intent upon his instruments and connections, replied rather pettishly that all was well and his companion had nothing to fear. Therefore Mathews just got on with driving his aeroplane. He took it well away from the aerodrome over the neighbouring jungle, climbing steadily the whole time. From that point the story belongs to McCandlish alone.

Since it will be remembered that he had undertaken the trip to find out one thing, and one thing only, it will be understood that he was concentrating with single-mindedness. When the aircraft's nose suddenly lurched down, with the result that his feet momentarily became airborne, Sergeant McCandlish was a little surprised. For the first time he looked out and all around him. He marked the height at which they were flying—which indeed was nowhere near what he held to be necessary for 'dive-bombing'. To put the thing in a nutshell, he could not make out just what was to do.

Still, he didn't wish to appear inquisitive. Pilots, it is well known, are inclined to be touchy. There was also the fact that although McCandlish was fond of flying he lacked a very great deal of experience in that art. Against this, however, he had evidence which carried weight to a man of normal common sense. It appeared that they were undoubtedly in close proximity to enemy lines, and although he had not heard any firing, the aircraft was still behaving in a peculiar manner. Having finished its lurching dive, it suddenly reared upwards, climbed to the point of stall, and then began to shudder and shake in alarming fashion.

McCandlish switched his mike on and inquired politely what the hell Mathews thought he was doing. The aircraft was now vibrating heavily, the intercom was uncertain and full of crackles and he couldn't clearly make out the reply. He started fiddling with the instrument to try and clear it while the aircraft seemed to be shaking its rivets loose. Then, through the noise and crackle, he heard Mathews shout, "Bale out!"

"Out?" roared McCandlish. "Why? What the hell's up with the kite?"

Through the hubbub and uproar of the intercom he heard Mathews repeat the order, and at the same time he caught a glimpse of something happening in front of him. It seemed as though Mathews was preparing to bale out himself, and was heaving up and pointing over the side.

McCandlish decided that it was no time for argument. The aircraft was not very high and if his pilot was to have a chance of jumping safely there must be no delay. Mathews would naturally wait until he had gone.

Hurriedly he slapped his tin hat, helmet and test equipment on the table before him. In his own words: "I had brought my tin hat along in case I was sick. I thought it might come in useful." Then he swung his seat round and crawled out over the side into the fierce draught of the slip-stream, keeping as close to the fuselage as possible.

This was the correct drill which he had carefully mugged up in the instruction books beforehand. But he was remembering now that most rear-gunners in the Squadron held that no one could get out of that type of aircraft without hitting the tailplane. As he launched himself clear he instinctively braced himself and looked towards the tail—but in actual fact didn't even see it and never knew whether its passing was close. Then he counted three, pulled his ring, and was rather surprised at feeling no horror of falling, only a sensation of floating gently in mid-air. A sudden crack from above and a jerk upon his body-harness put an end to that, however, and he looked up to see the broad white canopy of his parachute and to feel himself firmly supported. Whereupon he heard himself remark, quite loudly : 'Well done, Mac !'

Now the vast undulating area of the jungle was spread out below him in a variegated mass of greens and browns; and he wondered just how many hostile eyes were watching his approach out of the skies, and how many rifles were pointed in his direction, waiting for him to get within range. As he spotted the aircraft some distance away, he realized that even if Mathews managed to jump they'd have a job to find each other once they reached the ground. He looked round, trying to fix upon a landmark. He saw a hut on one of the hillsides, and decided to try and side-slip his parachute towards it.

Before he could do so the ground started its sudden, final rush up towards him and a second later he was down amongst the branches of the trees, crashing through them with a fine flurry and uproar of smashing twigs and foliage. When next he had any clear idea of what was happening he found himself lying flat on his back in a patch of elephant grass, gasping and panting, but thankful to be alive.

A few seconds afterwards he heard the drone of an aircraft circling immediately overhead. It was a familiar noise and he wondered if some other pilot of 45 Squadron had seen him and Mathews baling out in their parachutes . . . or had possibly seen the aircraft crash into the jungle.

He pulled himself together, struggled through the grass to a convenient tree, and climbed up until he could get a clear view of the sky above. Then, to his absolute astonishment, he saw the aircraft in which he had just been flying. There was no doubt about it. The number was perfectly clear and since it was flying low in a circle, obviously looking for him, it must be that Flight Sergeant Mathews was still at the controls.

McCandlish nearly fell out of his tree. Why he had been ordered to bale out—what had happened to the machine in the first place—how it had managed to get over all its troubles—were questions that raced through his mind. But since there was no hope of getting any answer, he decided that the most important thing to do was to make his exact position known. Therefore he locked his legs round the tree, tore a strip out of his shirt and started waving and hallooing violently.

Evidently Mathews saw him, for the aircraft swung round in his direction, swooped low over his head and then circled round to repeat the performance. Each time it passed, Mathews threw something out. Afterwards McCandlish learned that these things were a jungle-kit and a first-aid kit, but in any case they fell more than thirty yards away in the thick jungle, in grass which he already knew reached well above his head. He guessed he'd be lucky if he found either of them, which he didn't.

After this the machine turned and droned away, evidently taking a course straight back to base. By that time it was late afternoon, so McCandlish decided to head for the hut he had seen when he was coming down, and also to leave his spread parachute where it lay as a landmark in case he had to return to the spot. But getting through the jungle was no easier than he had imagined it would be. The tall elephant grass kept wrapping itself around him and making tangles beneath which he had to crawl or else plunge and stagger over the top of them. At last, however, he came to a clearing which he guessed would have been Mathews' target when dropping his life-saving supplies. He scouted round for some time but all he could find was the lid of a tin. Since it was bright and polished, he put it in his pocket, thinking that it might possibly come in useful as a heliograph. He set off again down a rough track, but stopped dead when he heard voices approaching.

Whether they were friends or enemies he had no idea, since he had no means of telling whether he was on his own or the enemy's side of the lines. With commendable prudence he jerked out all his available money and stowed it in his socks. A party of natives carrying heavy sticks came into sight along the trail.

They were tough-looking men, but although he could only understand one word in about fifty of their language, he realized with relief that they were disposed to be friendly. The leader pointed in the direction where he had left his parachute and told off some of his party whom McCandlish guessed were to fetch it. He gestured and led the way through the jungle in the opposite direction for about half a mile to a native village. A crowd was already gathered, in the middle of which an old grey-haired patriarch stood forward. He salaamed solemnly and McCandlish did the same, by now feeling faint and rather sick. Heavy reaction from his adventure had set in, and since he thought he might suddenly fall flat on his face, he sat down there and then on the ground.

The patriarch shouted an order and at once a mat was brought for him together with a brass bowl of some white, milky fluid which he tried and found tasted like a mixture of soap-suds and weak beer. However, he got some down politely and since he suddenly felt hungry, he used the native word for fruit. As a result, there was a scurrying amongst the natives and he found himself surrounded with bananas, tangerines and two large pine-apples.

By that time, what seemed to be the population of the whole village was standing around him in a circle, and he realized that it was probably the most entertaining thing that had happened to them for years. The women, who at first had hung in the background, now pushed their way to the front and stood chattering and giggling, most of them nursing babies at their breasts.

Although the natives obviously intended him no harm, McCandlish was hoping for some active help. He wanted to be put on a trail which would get him back to 45 Squadron and he wanted the trail to be a passable one. Therefore he decided to gain their friendship as quickly as possible. Remembering the tactics of his Member of Parliament at election times, he used the same principle. He got up and went to each mother in turn, pointed to her child and asked its name with an ingratiating smile. As the mother said the name he tried to repeat it as well as he could, and smilingly patted the child's head. Naturally, he made a hash of the pronunciation, but this was all to the good, for the women howled with laughter and some of the men began laughing too, and he was pressed to drink yet another bowl of beer-and-soap-suds.

While he pretended to be overjoyed with this hospitality, he started pointing in the direction he imagined the airfield to lie and indicated that he wanted to get there. He used what fragments of the language he knew. He made buzzing noises to imitate an aircraft, and spread his arms wide, sweeping round and pretending to land.

The natives chattered and seemed to understand him perfectly. Soon the patriarch picked three from the group, salaamed to him and indicated that they would take him upon his way. This in fact they did, even carrying him pick-a-back across streams and helping him up precipitous places until, after a long drag uphill, he was overjoyed to see a civilized building ahead. It was a charming European-type bungalow, and when the natives had knocked on the door an equally charming lady opened it in answer, and proved to be the wife of the District Officer.

McCandlish was invited in and given a meal forthwith, after which a native Warrant Officer of the Indian

Engineers, who had evidently been warned of his presence, arrived to take him over. The Warrant Officer led him in front of the local Chief of Police, by whom he was interrogated very closely. After his story had been taken down in detail, the native policeman asked the magnificent question, "But I do not understand why you jumped out of the aeroplane. Did you have a domestic quarrel with your pilot?"

At length, apparently satisfied, the policeman passed him on to an Engineers' section stationed alongside a nearby railway, where he spent the night and was given breakfast in the Officers' Mess. During the meal a difficult moment arose. McCandlish was given a plate of porridge, and not seeing any salt around, he ate it as it was. Immediately one of the Indian officers snapped suspiciously: "I have always understood, sir, that Scotsmen took salt with their porridge." McCandlish looked round the table and saw suspicion written on every face. When he answered that he felt it would be impolite to ask for salt—and when he ate it with obvious relish on his porridge when some was supplied—he was relieved to see all suspicion clear away.

Later that day, after a rail journey, McCandlish was restored to the bosom of 45 Squadron and to his own sleeping-hut in which Flight Sergeant Mathews occupied the next bed. Mathews was obviously delighted to see him safe and sound, but after greetings both of them spoke simultaneously.

"Why the hell did you go over the side?" inquired Mathews.

"What the hell happened? Why did you order me to jump?" asked McCandlish.

Said Mathews: "*Jump?* I never ordered you to jump! I'd had a bit of bother with the kite and I heard you trying to get through on the intercom so I shouted 'all right'. I kept on shouting 'all right'. I was waving at you from the front so you could see that all was well."

McCandish sat down heavily on his bed. The realization came to him that in certain circumstances the words 'all right' shouted by an excited New Zealand pilot over a bad intercom to a worried Scottish ground-airman can sound just like 'bale out'.

His only worry was that his Squadron Commander might not be prepared to believe that such a thing could happen, and he wondered just how heavy and awful the penalties might possibly be. He need not have worried, however, for the Commanding Officer, having heard the evidence and cross-questioned him carefully, sat back in his chair and roared with laughter.

His only remark was 'Good show!'; he being wise enough to know that a man who was obviously not an intending deserter would certainly never take to a parachute at a point which was perilously near enemy territory.

Meanwhile, Sergeant McCandlish is justifiably proud of the little gold caterpillar brooch he received from the Irvin Parachute Company designating him a member of a club which very few Service men who have not served as aircrew have been able to join.

9

THE STORY OF SIR BASIL EMBRY

In this book I have discussed men of courage. Words like 'heroic' or even 'brave' are generally detested by RAF personnel because they have so often been hysterically misused.

Yet I have known heroic men in my years with the Service, and I am prepared to use the adjective in regard to those men who have pressed home attack in circumstances which they knew meant certain death. I will also use it to describe men who have, knowingly, gone to certain death in order that their comrades might survive.

However, apart from this superlative word, I have found that any ordinary man of common sense will pull out of the bag a high standard of bravery whenever it becomes necessary (but may be that is because the RAF has always demanded a fairly high standard in what it calls 'ordinary').

All this brings me to Air Chief Marshal Sir Basil Edward Embry, KCB, KBE, former Commander in Chief of the Allied Air Forces in Central Europe, who has three bars to his Distinguished Service Order in addition to a Distinguished Flying Cross and an Air Force Cross.

Every man who has ever worn a light blue uniform during the last twenty years knows that name. No account of parachute jumping in the Second World War could be complete without Basil Embry's story. So here it is.

On May 27th, 1940, when the German blitzkrieg had carried the Nazi forces past the Maginot Line and down to the Channel ports, things were looking parlous for Britain. The Low Countries had fallen, and the trench system of 1914–18, perpetuated in concrete by General Maginot, had proved to be nothing but a tragically-expensive dream of defence. Our armies were in retreat on French soil, overwhelmed by gigantic odds. Dunkirk was to come. The Battle of Britain was to come. Meanwhile, the men in the forces still left to us could only fight on, confident of one thing—we might be wiped out, but we would never surrender.

On that May 27th, the then Wing Commander Embry commanded 107 Squadron of Blenheim MkIV bombers at Wattisham, which, in its entity as a Royal Air Force station, was under the command of the famous long-distance pilot, Group Captain Oswald Gayford. Embry was in an uncertain state of mind. He had that morning received a signal posting him to the command of RAF West Raynham with the acting rank of Group Captain —with immediate effect. This, of course, meant promotion, which is sweet to any ambitious man who is keen on his job. On the other hand, his present job meant a great deal more to Embry than the sudden promotion which is to be expected in wartime conditions. He had a fine squadron and he knew it. He had trained them hard and forged them into the sort of first-class unit of which every leader dreams. As a man of common sense he knew that the great battles of the war in the air were yet to be fought, and he did not relish 'being out of it' even so far as a Station Commander of high rank might be forced to be.

In accordance with orders, however, he formally handed over command to Acting Wing Commander L. R. Stokes; but that afternoon he decided to lead the Squadron, personally, in a sortie over the Fôret d'Hesdin. It was a lively raid, the flak was brisk, and the Squadron returned well peppered, but without casualties. First thing next morning orders came through for 107 Squadron to attack advancing enemy columns in the St Omer district.

This Embry could not resist. He privately arranged with Stokes that he would make this his last job, and both brief the boys and lead them in the attack. Stokes naturally bowed to higher authority. At four o'clock that afternoon, after Embry's briefing, Stokes took off leading the second vic formation of aircraft directly behind Embry's 'box' of three Blenheims. There was a crew of three in each aircraft—the pilot; the navigator, whose seat was slightly ahead and to the right; and the air-gunner, who resided in a power-operated gun-turret situated in the mid-upper part of the fuselage. Each Blenheim carried four bombs.

On Embry's orders the whole Squadron was to keep close formation and watch him, ready to follow in any evolution. They droned away over the gardens of Kent and over the silver expanse of the Channel which gleamed in the bright sunlight. Soon a grim pall of smoke showed on French ground, ahead. Embry's altimeter indicated 6000 feet as Calais slid below. Part of the town was burning, and a ship lay sinking in the harbour. In Embry's Blenheim Pilot Officer Tom Whiting was in the navigator's seat. Corporal Lang, his air-gunner was up in the mid-fuselage turret. Embry watched carefully and, still at the same altitude, realized that a German column was coming along a forest road, from the dust clouds which were rising.

This was just the target he had come to find. Embry put the nose of his aircraft down and led the Squadron into the attack, although he guessed that the Germans would be well supplied with mobile anti-aircraft guns. That, however, was just part of the job in hand and not a factor which could be taken into consideration.

The German AA gunners were very much on the job that afternoon. As 107 Squadron went down to deliver its bomb load, 'stuff' came flying up around them with uncomfortable accuracy. Suddenly Embry's window blew inwards violently and he jumped as a splinter of perspex drove into his leg. At the same time the Blenheim shuddered to a direct hit squarely under the gunner's turret. Embry yanked at the stick to climb away—but found that control had gone.

The Blenheim lurched drunkenly and then nosed up into a climb but, with the stick slack in his hand, Embry knew that it was none of his doing. He also knew that in the next minute the machine might be in a headlong spin from which he would have no means of righting it before it crashed into the ground and killed all hands.

Naturally, therefore, he snapped the 'bale-out' order over the intercom, but in the same second realized that it had been shattered and was out of order. Instinctively, he shouted, but saw no movement which would indicate understanding on the part of his navigator.

Embry, always a man of straightforward action, therefore did the only common-sense thing, although there was no provision for it in King's Regulations and Air Force Instructions. He whipped off his tin hat and chucked it at the navigator's head. At the same time he ripped undone his safety harness and heaved up, to look round for the gunner.

Corporal Lang was sprawled dead over his controls. As far as that poor lad was concerned there was nothing that any aircraft captain could do.

Embry saw with relief, however, that Tom Whiting, his navigator, was very much alive—possibly by reason of the clout he had received from the steel helmet—and was bending down, wrenching at the escape hatch. Whilst this was happening the aircraft stalled and then heeled dizzily over on to its side. Embry steadied himself as best he could, saw that the hatch had come open, and realized that the aircraft had gone into a spin, and that there wasn't much time left. Whiting was hesitating about going out, probably because he was waiting for his junior in rank, Corporal Lang, to go first.

Once again Embry took emergency action. He planted a foot squarely on Whiting's bottom and kicked him headlong out of the aircraft. After that he went himself.

In the normal way of such things the aircraft disappeared forthwith, and he counted up to the normal 'three' before wrenching at his release ring. He felt the comforting pull of the harness webbing about his body as the parachute cracked open above his head.

He soon realized that he was going down straight into the general upheaval of battle. As he floated into the uproar he caught sight of his late aircraft and watched it spin-in and explode in an uprush of flame. Directly below him was the forest road and the German transport column, whose AA gunners seemed to be marking him as their general target. However, their aim did not seem so good now and he was not hit as he wrenched at his shroud-lines and side-slipped directly across the column, to land with a thud and roll head over heels in a field about 300 yards away.

Embry scrambled to his feet, cleared himself of his parachute and looked up to see his squadron of Blenheims reforming, obviously under the leadership of Stokes. He counted them and marked two missing from the number which had originally taken off. He saw them turning for home, hotly attacked by German fighters, but in fact all but two of the aircraft did get back to base without further casualties. Embry contacted Tom Whiting, who had also landed nearby, but waved to him to lie flat because at the same time he saw a German patrol approaching. As a result, while Embry was picked up, Whiting evaded immediate capture. But it was not to be for long—and he was forced to spend the rest of the war in a prison camp.

From that point onwards Embry's adventures were such as to make one of the most fantastic stories that ever came out of any war, but since it has been fully covered in several books[1], and so is generally well known in all its details, I will only give an outline of it here.

Embry managed to break away from the prisoner-of-war column into which he was herded. He was captured again, managed to steal a German rifle and clubbed three Germans senseless in winning to freedom a second time. Once more after this he was captured, and escaped yet again by the expedient of hiding in a farm manure-heap for six hours.

In the course of these adventures he operated on his own wounded leg, which, naturally, showed signs of poisoning, and removed the perspex splinter. In making for friendly lines (although in the chaotic state of the war he was not too sure where they were) he swam across the River Somme. He was nearly drowned in making his way across one of the local swamp regions. But eventu-

[1] e.g. *Wingless Victory*, a PAN Book.

ally he got to Paris and there he was amongst the silent crowds which watched the German forces make their entry into the city.

Cutting it all short, the indomitable Basil Embry finally got himself off the continent of Europe, back to England—and back to his old unit after the space of just over two months. On August 2nd of the same year, at Ipswich railway station, he got out of the train to find a hilarious reception committee of the officers of the Squadron under the leadership of Oswald Gayford.

From that point on Basil Embry reverted to normal duty as an Air Force officer on operations to the end of the war. He fought through the desert campaigns. He was posted home to command No2 Group RAF (the Group in which he was serving when he was shot down). He accumulated, by the end of hostilities, 4 DSOs, 1 DFC and 1 AFC, apart from the knighthood bestowed upon him by the late King George VI.

Before finally being entrusted with the leadership of the Allied Central European Air Forces, Sir Basil became Air Officer Commanding in Chief of Fighter Command—an appointment which, by his example, was held to be entirely fitting by every man who has ever flown in the Royal Air Force.

10

DAD'S THUNDERBOLT GOES IN

Mrs Bernard Wilson paused in the task of cutting a hedge and turned to look skywards, shading her eyes as she heard the drone of an aircraft approaching from the nearby Mersey River. Her young son Patrick was mowing the lawn a few yards away and for a few moments the clatter of the machine prevented him from hearing anything much else. As he turned where the lawn met the flower-beds near the house, he saw his mother's attitude. He stopped at once, listened, and then with all of a fourteen-year-old boy's keenness for things mechanical announced: "It's a Thunderbolt; that's the turbo-supercharger howling. That's Dad."

He grinned at the success of his ear-spotting as the tough, compact form of an American Lockheed Thunderbolt single-seater fighter came into view, going very fast and making a gentle dive over the house from a height of about 2000 feet.

As it passed, Mrs Wilson waved her garden shears cheerfully. In that aircraft, as it thundered on its way in the clear sunshine of a May morning in 1943, she knew that her husband, Bernard, was at the controls. As the machine climbed steeply into the inevitable Liverpool haze her heart felt a little uncertain, for she knew what was going to happen. Young Pat, however, was alive with excitement as he ran across the garden to her side. The Thunderbolt climbed high through the haze with the sun directly on it, and it wasn't often that young Pat managed to get such an excellent view of his father at work.

"He'll probably do some very hot dives now," he said. "Test out the elevator controls. Maybe he'll do some real aerobatics if he feels she's good."

For a few moments Mrs Wilson also watched the tiny shape of the fighter as it glinted in the sunlight and made a screaming dive before pulling out in a long, rising curve, the whine of the supercharger coming from the distant heights with all the curious effect of time-lag. Then she turned to give her attention to the hedge again. She never very much cared for watching her husband throwing a new aeroplane about the sky even though, as Chief Test Pilot to the Lockheed Organization at the airport, she knew him to be one of the safest and sanest pilots alive. Nevertheless, no woman ever entirely trusts high-speed machinery, especially when the father of her four children is moving at high speed with it.

She was also feeling a little keyed-up that afternoon. It was a long time since she had heard from their eldest boy, David, who was fighting in the Japanese campaign in Burma. Meanwhile, young Pat was hoping that the war would last another four years so that he, too, could get himself into an aeroplane and try his hand. She tried not to think about such things. The other two youngsters gave no worry for the time being. Young Bob was only eight and at school locally. Seventeen-year-old Jane had a job she liked on the telephone switchboard of the Lockheed Company at the airport where her father was stationed.

Mrs Wilson raised her shears to start work again and tried not to look at the Thunderbolt as it whined its way through a regulation, but highly spectacular, programme of evolutions. Then, with a sense of relief, she realized that the test was over, for the machine dropped down the sky to a level path and again passed directly over the house at about 2000 feet, taking a straight course for the airport.

As it passed her, however, and went directly towards the sun she suddenly saw a long trail of smoke pluming out from behind the tail. Mrs Wilson knew a lot about aeroplanes, as was natural, and her heart missed a beat. Any kind of irregular smoke from any kind of machine she knew as a peculiarly unpleasant phenomenon.

"What's that trail, Pat?" she asked, trying to keep her voice steady. "That—that smoke?"

Young Pat said "Vapour trail" in a small, sharp voice. He knew perfectly well the smoke wasn't vapour. He was lying on the spur of the moment to try and save his mother's feelings. "It's only vapour, Mother. I say, let's go inside. I'm tired of mowing the lawn. I—I want a drink of water."

Even as he was speaking, however, a vicious sparkle of flame gleamed in the smoke that was streaming from the aircraft. Then the note of the engine went up suddenly, and the Thunderbolt went up with it, leaving a long ugly trail of black. Flames were now clearly blasting round the fuselage as it roared high into the glare of the sun.

Mrs Wilson tried to speak, but couldn't. She saw young Pat standing rigid, his face dead white, as he watched his father's blazing machine climbing apparently out of control, up the sky. Mrs Wilson dropped the shears with a clatter upon the grass. She could not help shading her eyes and watching too. Without knowing it, she was saying, "He's on fire . . . Oh! Pat, he's on fire . . . he's on fire . . ."

In the dim heights of the haze they both saw the aircraft cartwheel over slowly. Their eyes were dazzled by the sunlight, but owing to the long, curling plume of smoke the tiny machine was clearly pinpointed in their view. Over the crest of the climb it went and then began falling. With smoke, sparks and bits of charred wreckage flying off, it dived down vertically, the engine still running at full throttle, the whine of the supercharger rising in cadence. It was giving out a banshee wail as the blazing fighter finished the last thousand feet or so of its power dive. There was a hissing crash as it finally smashed into the waters of the Mersey, and disappeared . . . then an uncanny silence.

Pat spoke first. Throughout his young life, his father had trained him in the stoic tradition of airmen. Whatever happens, don't panic. Keep your head. When the worst has happened, keep it all the more.

"It looks like the old man has had it," he said in as steady a voice as he could manage. Then—a first-class credit to his father's training—he walked steadily across the lawn, picked up the handle of the mower and started working again. In a choking silence his mother unsteadily bent down to pick up the shears and turned back to the hedge, although she could hardly see where it was. She knew that she must support the boy in the bravery of his

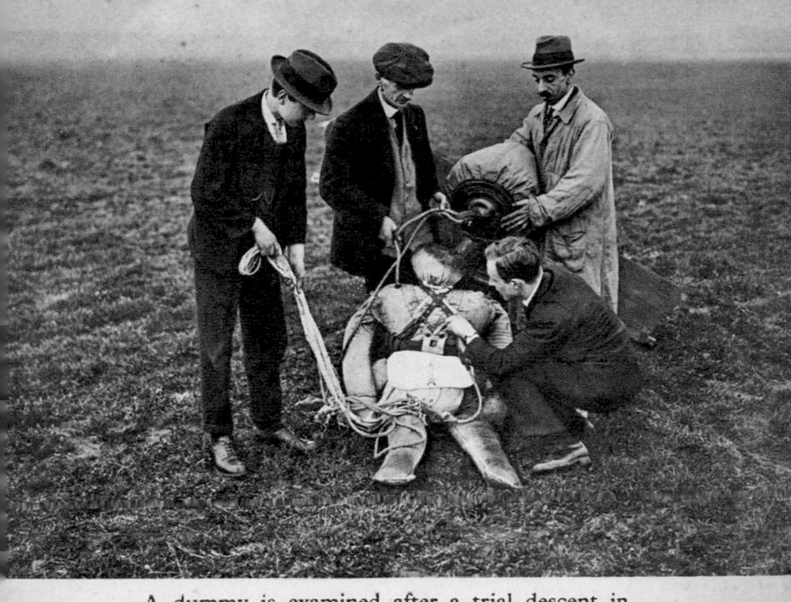

A dummy is examined after a trial descent in parachute tests at Croydon aerodrome, May 1922

Practising parachute 'pull off' at the RAF Parachute School, Henlow, before World War II

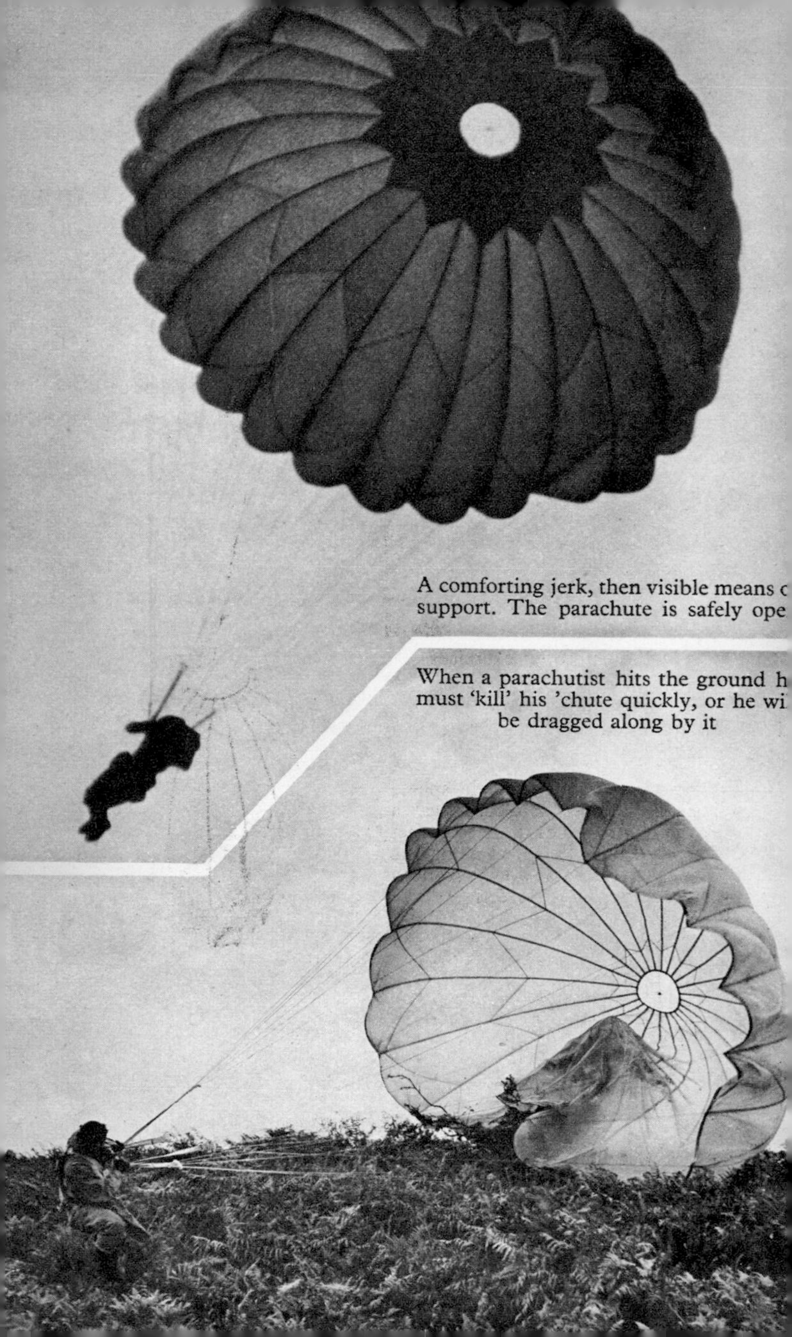

A comforting jerk, then visible means c
support. The parachute is safely ope

When a parachutist hits the ground h
must 'kill' his 'chute quickly, or he wi
be dragged along by it

Baling out during paratroop exercises

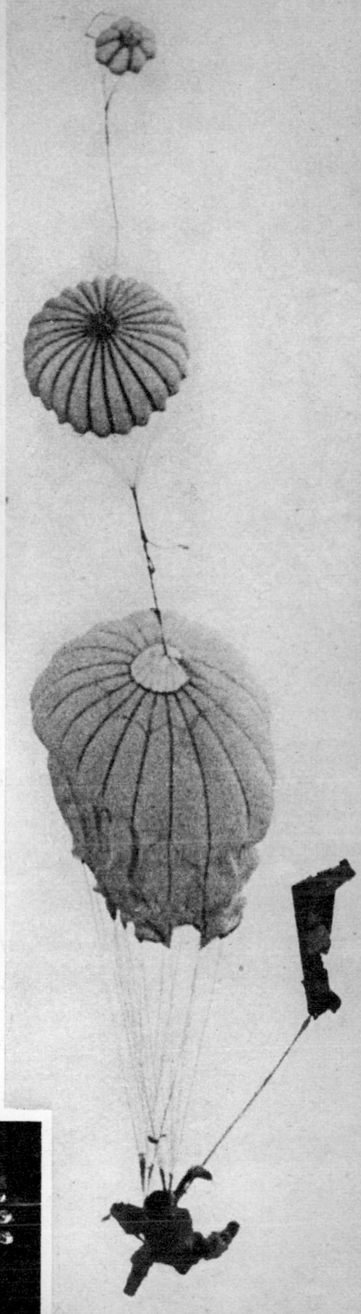

Low-level ejection at high speed: using the new 66-lb ejector-seat a dummy pilot leaves a Meteor jet fighter travelling at speed along the runway, and floats down from a height of only 20 ft.

The badge of the Caterpillar Club

Parachute packs in position, paratroopers march towards their transport plane during a training exercise

The British massed drop at Arnhem during World War II

act. There was in any case nothing that either of them could do. Nothing but wait for the ringing of the telephone bell in the house . . . and the ghastly news that some sympathetic voice would have to announce . . .

. . . . .

At the Lockheed telephone-switchboard young Jane Wilson was on duty alone. Work on the board had been fairly slack throughout the morning, but she knew her father was testing an aircraft. She heard the rising and falling wail of the turbo-supercharger, and once or twice tried to look out of the window in case she might get a sight of him. Then, as a light on the switchboard flickered for her attention, she heard the long whining drone of the aircraft in its last dive. No one who knows anything about aeroplanes likes a prolonged sound of that kind when it comes from too close to the ground. Jane connected her caller as quickly as she could, her heart fluttering as the roar came lower and lower. Then it stopped. The sudden cessation of the noise outside was ominous to her ears.

She tried to tell herself that all was well. Sound can often play queer tricks. It was possible that it was some other aircraft; not the one that her father was testing. In any case someone might have made a very low dive and then gone screaming away across the countryside so that some trick of the wind carried the rest of its engine noise well away.

A minute or so later all her hopes were dashed. The switchboard in front of her came alive with a rush. She forced herself to duty, but her hands were not steady as she plugged the connecting lines for each successive call. There were rapid demands for an ambulance—for warning to the Medical Officer—for the fire-engine crew to be turned out. Since she knew that even the delay of a second or so now might mean all the difference between getting a man out of a crash alive or dead, she dared ask no questions. But the grim question in her mind was soon answered. The sort of excitable typist who always seems to be handy on such occasions flung open the door and shouted at her, "Jane—Jane—your father's just crashed into the river."

Jane made no answer. At the first lull in the medley of calls, she carried on with her duty and rang the manager's office.

"Mr Walker," she asked as steadily as she could when she heard his crisp reply.

"Yes, Jane."

"Mr Walker, one of our aircraft has just crashed—into the river. I believe . . . I believe it's Dad . . ."

She heard the manager's sharp indrawing of breath.

"Oh, my dear girl," he said. "Look here, are you alone in there?"

But before she could answer she heard his voice raised as he called urgently at his secretary. "Audrey," he bellowed, "they've left that child Jane Wilson on the switchboard alone. Get her off. Get her off right now."

Jane was thankful to find herself relieved in the matter of half a minute. She was soon surrounded by friends who got busy with the making of a comforting cup of tea.

. . . . .

Test Pilot Bernard Wilson's experience in his Thunderbolt aircraft that day was lively. After taking off and having made the first routine tests of controls, he liked the machine and made his usual pass over his own house before climbing away confidently to carry out the more spectacular part of his job. In pilot's parlance he found everything 'very nice' as he climbed and dived. The controls answered firmly in all ways that were normal to the type, and no vices showed any hint of developing. Therefore he came down and set course for the airport to land and make his report as quickly as might be, so that he could get home to lunch.

But just after passing the house again at about 2000

feet there was a sudden loud bang from somewhere in the region of the engine. Dense smoke blew back, completely filling the cockpit, which immediately became almost unbearably hot. Wilson naturally reached up to grab the inner handle of the cockpit cover and wrench it open. But the cover wouldn't move. Almost blinded and breathing with difficulty, he tore at it for a moment, but then realized that if he was to have a chance of getting out alive he must get height, and lots of it—fast.

Partly by instruments, partly by sight and a great deal by good fortune, he kept the aircraft stable laterally as he pulled the stick back and held her in a climb. At around 7500 feet he won his battle with the cockpit canopy and finally wrenched it open. By that time flames from the engine were blasting back, and in the last few seconds before he got the cover open things were looking chancy. However, once the hood was open he whipped undone his safety harness and cockpit gear and went out over the side. The first thing he was conscious of as he went head over heels through the Liverpool haze was the nice, cool fresh air. For some reason he was not a bit bothered about his parachute, whether it would open, or whether the pack had got burnt at all, with possible disastrous results. His confidence was justified. He heard a crack over his head as the big silken envelope spread out and filled. Then a comforting jolt on his body harness, and he was floating down serenely with the vast relief map of Liverpool and the Mersey estuary and docks spread out below. Not very far away he saw the deserted Thunderbolt complete its cartwheel and go screaming down, leaving a long trail of fire and smoke until it finally smashed into the waters of the river.

Wilson examined the river carefully, made a rough estimate of the spot in which he was going to land, and saw that what shipping there was in movement did not appear to be going anywhere in that direction. Still he was not unduly worried. In the clear sunshine he knew he must be a conspicuous object coming down on his parachute and there was not the slightest doubt that he would be seen. Indeed it was more than probable that boats were getting under way from one or other of the quays already to pick him up. Meanwhile, he had no bothers in his mind about his wife and family. Although they had probably seen the crash they must have seen him getting out, and now that his parachute was open their minds should surely be at rest. In this he was entirely wrong. The haze and the sun-glare prevented anyone on the north side of the river either from seeing him leave the aircraft, or from spotting the earlier part of his leisurely journey earthwards when the parachute opened. Mrs Wilson and young Pat went inside the house not long after the aircraft had struck the water.

When Wilson came to take his ducking he went through the emergency drill in which every airman is carefully rehearsed. He turned the swivel release just before he struck the water, and knocked it undone as he broke the surface. This rid him of the danger of being dragged down by the harness and shroud lines and left him free to swim. But he had to swim for quite a while before he saw the slightest signs of rescue coming his way.

Only when he was feeling very tired, and considerably frightened, did he at last spot the boat which came plunging alongside with men leaning over the gunwale to get a grip on his flying-suit and haul him aboard.

. . . . .

Within the Wilson household the arrival home from school of Bob, the youngest, caused something of a sensation, which the cheerful eight-year-old obviously expected and thoroughly enjoyed.

"Somebody's just baled out of a Thunderbolt," he said. "I saw him coming down when I was at the bus stop. Say, do you think it's Daddy?"

Mrs Wilson hardly believed her ears. "Bobby, are you

sure?" she asked urgently. "You really saw it? You saw a man in a parachute—*yourself*?"

"I certainly did," said Bob, purposely trying to be nonchalant in his importance. "I watched him come down right into the water."

"The water!" echoed Mrs Wilson and Pat.

"Sure, in the river," said Bob. "If it's Dad that's where he is. They were sending boats out for him right away."

The elder boy and his mother stared at each other. Still they hardly dared to hope. Then at last came a call from Jane at the airport. Even after that, since the message gave no certainty, they hardly knew what to believe until a car drew up and out of it stepped a damp, smoke-blackened but cheerfully grinning paterfamilias who was the centre of a rush from his wife and family directly he entered the garden gate. The welcome was joined by Jane, who had been driven home from the airfield and arrived almost at the same time.

But, as is the way of airmen, Wilson had little to say about his adventure to the newspaper-men who, naturally enough, soon put in an appearance.

"There's no need to make a fuss," he said. "If you make a living testing aircraft, maybe you'll have to leave an aircraft sometime." He glanced at his family with a grin. "Still," he finished, "I'm certainly sorry that on this occasion everyone *had* to get into the act!"

11

A JUMP TO MEET THE RUSSIANS

WHEN twenty-one-year-old Bernard John Kemp joined the Royal Air Force in May 1940 he 'put in' for an observer's course, although it was his ambition to be a pilot. Above that ambition, however, was an impatient desire to get really flying and into the war. The authorities had informed him: "You can get an observer's course in six months, but you will have to wait a year to go for pilot."

Kemp, therefore, went through all the normal routine agony of the Initial Training Wings at Hastings, and the observer's course at Prestwick. Completing training at Louth in Lincolnshire on the first course to be held there, he remembers with some vividness the remark made by the officer who finally pinned upon him his observer's brevet. Said the officer: "This is too easy. If I had my way, you chaps would do ten operational trips before you got one of these."

Precisely why any member of an aircrew, except the pilot, should be denied a brevet before having 'gone operational' escapes the writer of this chronicle, just as it did Kemp. Still these things happen in the best-regulated of Services, and it is not much to worry about. The officer concerned, however, needn't have worried about young Mr Kemp's justification of his badge in any way whatever. He was shortly to have more excitement than is normally crammed into ten operational trips, however arduous.

At twenty-one he was—as indeed he still is—a quick-thinking, highly imaginative chap with a keen sense of observation. In the early days of his operational flying, he noticed that some of the girls around, locally known as 'chop' girls, seemed to have a 'jinx' on aircrews. More than one of them was known to have been the special girl-friend of quite a string of men who went off in their aircraft and never came back. Kemp chuckled as he told me that he forced himself to go out with the one who had the most impressive list, just to show he wasn't scared . . . and felt as jumpy as the devil about it for some time afterwards.

Meanwhile, he was keen on his job, and found astro-navigation absorbingly interesting. Much of the time when the other boys were beating things up at dances or at parties, he would be hanging out of the window of his billet, shooting star positions with his sextant.

As a result of this practice, there came a certain evening when he was the only man of the Squadron to get his aircraft over its objective (Berlin) on time. The rest of the 400 on the raid were delayed in reaching the target area owing to inaccurate wind-forecasting. Kemp also brought the aircraft another distinction which was not so much appreciated by his comrades. But of that more later.

The date of the raid was September 7th, 1941, and the time of take-off 8.15 pm. Fortunately, it was a warm, balmy evening because Kemp's lively imagination had been bothering him. When he went to draw his Irvin suit, he noticed that the storekeeper had issued him with a second-hand one on which was marked the name of a man he knew to be dead. He tried to hand it back and asked for another, but the storekeeper inquired what all the bother was about, and was there anything in that to make anyone windy? To accept any such suggestion, or admit it even by inference, was more than any twenty-one-year-old of self-respect could face. Kemp, therefore, took the dead man's suit without another word and went off. But he didn't take it to the aeroplane. He stuffed it in a kit-bag in his quarters, and left it there when the time came to take the air.

At that time he was a seasoned man with seven completed operations behind him. He wasn't suffering from 'beginner's twitch' and, as he went out to the aircraft at its dispersal, he was in a normal frame of mind. There is a normality which men can and do develop in their attitude to the dangers, uncertainties and hazards of the sort of thing Kemp was facing. Nobody could say that it is a happy or cheerful normality, even though the man concerned can appear to be so outwardly. Very few sane, balanced men, while waiting to start such a job, can entirely forget the fact that they are probably never going to come back to the familiar sights, smells and sounds of the aerodrome they are about to leave, or the girl-friends, the wives and children who loom so importantly in the background of their lives.

Some men hide their feelings by a rather flamboyant form of bravado, by cheerful swearing and laughter during the preliminary stages of making ready to start. Others are silent. The leaders usually get over the worst of the strain by necessary preoccupation with the detail work that goes with the responsibility.

Kemp was probably one of the most normal types of people you could have found in circumstances of this kind. By this I mean he has a stable character. He does not regard himself as any form of a hero, and would be both horrified and embarrassed if anybody suggested any such thing. In short, he is of a type which, by good fortune, these islands breed in large numbers. Men able to stand up to intense nervous strain for long periods because of a deep conviction that that is neither more nor less than 'what any ordinary bloke can be expected to do'.

Nevertheless, a lively imagination is not always a pleasant thing to have, and once again that evening Kemp found his own inconvenient. As the big Whitley aircraft started rolling and then began to gather speed down the runway, he saw a line of people standing at the grass edge. Undoubtedly they were just the ordinary people who either by duty or normal curiosity are on hand at any time of operational take-off in war. But, as the aircraft gathered speed and flashed past them, Kemp saw that they were all waving, and he had a sudden desolate conviction that they were waving the aircraft and its crew a final farewell.

Those who like to deal in omens may find food for thought in this. Kemp admits that he never remembers having had that impression on any previous take-off. He will admit that if the flight had ended differently he might have forgotten the incident altogether. He excuses himself by saying that at the time he was 'a bit keyed up', or the point at which the stable man finds added strength and the unstable has hysterics.

From that point, however, Kemp was far too occupied with the business in hand to let omens and superstitions trouble him. The aircraft had as heavy a bomb load as was possible for its long trip to Berlin and back. It was carrying two 1000-pound bombs, four 500-pounders and a rack of sixty incendiaries weighing four pounds each. By modern standards, indeed by later standards of the war, such a load was a pip-squeak. But the Whitley aircraft had been designed long before war broke out, when targets at such a range as Berlin were not thought of seriously as objectives. Meanwhile, Kemp concentrated on his navigation and, as I have said before, the final result repaid all his skill.

The Whitley arrived over the city dead on briefing time—11.55 pm. It was the only aircraft of the Squadron to get there with such perfect punctuality. But, directly it arrived, the welcome it received from the ground gunners was more than enthusiastic.

As the pilot steadied the machine to make the run-up to his target, Kemp was conscious of a tremendous noise of bursting flak all around; constant flashing explosions and clouds of smoke wreathing back in the strong moonlight. The reception was as hot as he had yet known in his experience, and he privately reckoned that they were going to be lucky if they got away without serious damage after they had spotted their precise target and dropped their load.

Then, suddenly, he reared violently in his seat and hardly knew what had happened when he found he had collapsed back again. The first sensation had been as though some unseen giant had given him a terrific kick in the backside, but apart from the stunning impact which knocked his senses askew, he felt no pain. He realized he was bleeding, and a gingerly investigation showed him that he had been wounded in the right buttock.

This was unpleasant, but as he began mentally to 'get back' to his surroundings, he realized something that was positively uncanny. All the noise, which had previously been so deafening, had now stopped. There was an eerie silence. It was suddenly borne in upon him that even the engines had stopped their strong, heavy drone.

For a moment he had the unreal impression that the aircraft was empty. Then he saw that the pilot and co-pilot were still in their seats. At the same time he realized that the plug which connected his helmet ear-phones with the intercom was dangling clear. He saw that, in the wild jerk he gave after being wounded, he must have dragged the plug out of its socket. And as a result he had not heard his pilot's order, which had obviously been given, for the crew to bale out.

As clear thinking came back to him, Kemp decided that since the disabled and impotent aircraft was plumb over the centre of the city of Berlin, it was time for him to see that the object of the flight was carried out. Therefore he released the bombs. As the aircraft lifted to the loss of their weight, he saw the second-pilot throwing him down his parachute pack. After which the 'second-dickie' took a firm hold of his own release ring and dived away.

Kemp dragged himself close to the captain's seat and yelled out to know if there was anything he could do. The captain had his feet braced up in the 'crash' position. He shouted back that there was nothing anyone could do and told Kemp to get away as quickly as he could.

In circumstances of this kind it is a junior's duty to obey orders as quickly as he can, and so give his senior a chance of life as 'the last to leave'. Kemp dropped down to sit on the edge of the escape hatch with his feet dangling into space while he tried to tighten his straps. He took a dive, but jerked at his rip-cord almost too soon. As he turned head over heels in space he had the alarming sight of his pilot-chute narrowly missing the tailplane of the aircraft as it whisked overhead. A few minutes later his captain was dead, killed in the final crash when the aircraft struck the ground and disintegrated in flames.

Meanwhile, for a few moments, Kemp went through a spasm of rather sickening pain. This was because the parachute harness around his body was looser than it should have been; the result of wearing no Irvin suit, because he would not wear one that had belonged to a dead man. The webs of the harness which passed down between his thighs therefore caught him awkwardly when the speed of his free fall was checked by the opening envelope above. The resulting pain was just as bad as many a rugger player or cricketer has had cause to remember. When a man's weight is almost entirely depending upon thigh-straps of this kind, it isn't too easy to alter position and gain relief. Kemp heaved and hauled himself on his shoulder-straps as best he could, through sickening moments until he found some sort of ease.

He realized that he was as brightly lit up as any music-hall star on the stage of the Palladium. First, one searchlight found him. Then, as it steadied on the white mushroom of his parachute, others came swinging in vast sweeps across the sky to join the focus of the first. The pyramid of searchlights gradually followed Kemp down to the ground. He had a feeling of helpless nakedness in that glare as he came down the last few thousand feet. The AA guns were now thudding and banging a ferocious chorus all over the city as the rest of the raiders began dropping their bomb loads. As the vague darkness of the ground approached, he tensed himself, waiting for the sudden barking of machine-guns, which he more than half expected would open up and riddle him with bullets when he came within range.

However, for once the German gunners restrained their well-known sense of humour. Not a shot was fired at him as he dropped down below the trajectory of the searchlight beams and fell quickly into what appeared like a mass of sea anemones, an area of thin, waving fronds which seemed to reach out to grasp him.

Kemp used his common sense and decided that it must be a forest. But it wasn't. As an example of the extraordinary tricks that the eyes of a sorely-strained man can play, it was just ordinary medium-length grass, with very hard, solid earth directly beneath it. Kemp hit the earth with a force that knocked the breath out of him, long before he reckoned he was within 20 feet of it. The thud caused him to bite his lip, heavily and painfully. But he still kept his head, plunged and struggled to free himself of his parachute harness before dropping down, relaxed, to regain his breath.

He was very quickly surrounded by a group of men who had evidently watched his descent in the searchlight display and were ready at his point of landing. From what he could see of their dress, they were farm workers. They treated him decently enough, helping him down into the cellar of a house nearby, where they were soon joined by some of the women of the establishment.

The place where Kemp had landed was just east of Berlin, in agricultural country. He spoke very little German, but found it easy enough to make the farm folk understand that he was wounded. One of the men glanced at his bloodstained seat and gestured to him to take his trousers down, but this he refused to do in front of the women. Somehow, there was a difference between making a public show of oneself and being treated by a trained hospital nurse. Both the men and the women seemed amused at his modesty, but they helped him to another cellar where a couple of the men undressed him. Then one of the women appeared with hot water and rough bandages, and did her best for him while he was lying on his face.

This woman earned his undying gratitude, for, during the four hours that he stayed there, and before men of the Luftwaffe arrived to take him away, she smuggled some chocolate to him. The men treated him decently too, to his surprise. They all gave him cigarettes, and when he indicated he was hungry, brought him black bread, a coarse jam and some ersatz coffee, which was peculiarly bitter to his tongue. Apparently there was no sugar or milk available.

At last, a very young and smart officer of the Luftwaffe put in an appearance, and saluted him with considerable ceremony. This man spoke fair English, and remained just as polite and pleasant when Kemp announced that he was a sergeant and not the holder of a commission.

Throughout all this the shrewd Kemp suspected the usual build up in which the confidence of captured men was very carefully gained by pleasant treatment in order that they might be persuaded to talk. He was not far wrong, for after humane treatment of his wounds he was taken to Dulag Luft, near Frankfort-on-Main, where, after refusing to give more than his name and number, according to regulations, he was forthwith clapped into solitary confinement. Here he got very thirsty and asked for water. The guards brought him a rough-looking wine, but having heard about such things, he refused to drink it, knowing that it probably contained a relaxing drug that would put him off his guard. Later on he discovered that others were given the same treatment but made the mistake of drinking the wine and realized they had said much more than was necessary, even to discussing the type of aeroplanes in which they had been flying. It is a measure of Kemp's character that, even after three years in prison camp, he was still periodically up for questioning and never disclosed any further details.

Of his life in prison camp throughout the years that followed, Kemp has little to say, other than a general description given by most men who have endured it. "Oh, well—it was hell, but somehow we got through."

Nevertheless, there is part of Kemp's prison experiences which I think has its place within these covers, and which concerns a period right at the end of hostilities when his German guards actually volunteered to be prisoners themselves, and put their British ex-captives in charge.

Kemp spent three and a half years in a number of different prison camps, ending up at Stalag Luft 1, at Barth near the Baltic coast in Pomerania. Here, about two months before the end of the war, the rumour reached the RAF prisoners that orders had been issued by the Nazi headquarters that all captured flying men were to be 'eliminated'.

Accordingly, they secretly gathered up arms and ammunition under the noses of their guards, who were becoming lethargic and hopeless. In any case, no attempt was ever made to put the order into effect. As time went on it became plain that the Russians would be first of the two great forces which would reach Barth. The boys were amused by one of their number who hung out of his window every night bellowing 'Come on, Joe', and were even more diverted when a German guard asked them to keep quiet and make him stop howling 'Let me out'.

As the days passed, they began to hear firing and realized that they might be sandwiched between the Russian and the Allied armies and their siege guns! However, on the day they heard over their home-made radios that the Russians had finally broken the Kustrin bridgehead, all sounds of firing ceased. Meanwhile, squadrons of aircraft were taking off from the German aerodrome only two miles away from the camp. The evacuation continued by night, the aircraft carrying no navigation lights, probably because Russian fighters were in the vicinity.

The prisoners began to hear explosions at the aerodrome. These became incessant and it was obvious that the local German Luftwaffe were destroying everything in the process of pulling out. The prisoners stood on incinerators in the camp watching the fireworks, the detonations becoming so heavy that some of them set to work to dig slit-trenches.

It was two o'clock on the morning of May 1st that they suddenly heard a rumble of carts and transport in the German quarters of the camp. A little later the sleepless prisoners saw the vague silhouettes of men gathering and leaving the camp at the gate of their barracks. There was a pause and a few soft whistles. Suddenly there was yelling and cheering and the searchlights were switched on in the camp guard-boxes.

The prisoners realized that the guards had gone and that some of their friends were already up in the boxes having fun with the lights. The camp was theirs.

On the morning of May 1st the imaginative Kemp gained a deep enjoyment from two things. The first was that the day, as he knew well, was officially 'the day of national celebration for the German people'. The second was an astonishing announcement, read out to them on parade by their own Wing Commander. This stated that the RAF prisoners had changed places with the Germans, many of whom were still left. The Germans had agreed that they were now prisoners, and their ex-captives guards. Meanwhile, the Wing Commander announced, typically enough, that the new prisoners-of-war were to be treated honourably, in strict conformation with the rules set down in the Geneva Convention (rules that had never bothered the Germans overmuch). He announced that, as from that moment, military law was to be enforced with the usual heavy penalties for looting or anything of the kind.

Thereafter it was typical of any British Command that, although the camp had changed hands, there was no noticeable change of routine. The ex-prisoners moved over into the German quarters, and were delighted by their comfort, very different from their previous conditions in which twenty men had been cramped into a

25-by-15-foot room. Next day a platoon of ex-prisoners was detailed to go to the nearby aerodrome, take it if necessary from any Luftwaffe men who were still there, or meet and fraternize with the Russians. They were armed with heavy German machine guns, taken from their mountings in the guard boxes, and with rifles. Again their main orders were typically British. If there were Russians who saw them and fired by mistake, they were not to fire back.

On the way they were amused that the local German civilians were having slight difficulty in deciding whom to welcome. Russian and American as well as white flags were hanging from the local houses. Kemp reflected that these were the same people who, only a year ago, had stood about as they were marched past and spat at them, calling them *Terrorfleigers* and *Schweinerei*.

On the way, however, they heard the sudden heavy roar of tanks and thought them to be an SS Panzer Division in retreat. There were ten in all and they thundered down the road into Barth; the boys could hear the uproar of their machine guns firing.

When the party got to the aerodrome they found the place practically deserted. One depressed German soldier was wandering around, but he took not the slightest notice of them and they left him alone. In the nearby railway siding they spotted a 200-pound bomb wired up to a petrol wagon, and with their minds alerted for booby-traps, they gave it a wide berth. Then their officers went up into the control tower, and whilst the men were setting up guns in pits, Verey cartridges were fired to let those at the camp know that all was well. An hour later the little British force saw an amazing sight. They heard a rumbling in the distance and then on the skyline saw a long line of horse-drawn vehicles almost exactly like a western covered-wagon train out of a cowboy film.

When they realized that this was the approach of the Russian forces—the advance guard of the much-publicized Red Army—they could hardly believe it. However, the fact remained, and after two of their number, with a Russian interpreter, had gone out to make contact with the approaching troops, a small, green four-seater saloon appeared, driving fast on to the aerodrome. It stopped near a gun-pit and out poured Russians. They shouted, flung their arms wide, and a moment later the RAF boys were all round them slapping backs, shaking hands and yelling '*Tovarish*' and anything else of a Russian nature that sounded friendly which they could think of.

Next day, May 3rd, after a long consultation between their Commander and the Russians, it was agreed that the RAF should occupy the airfield until such time as aircraft arrived to carry them home to England. It was clearly understood, however, that everything—arms, cars, etc.—they had commandeered was to be regarded merely as a loan and was to be returned to the Russians in perfect condition when they finally left.

From then until the official Armistice Day, May 8th, the RAF boys found little to do. They rode around the countryside armed with tins of margarine and coffee which they bartered for livestock and dairy produce. One enterprising lad got a perfectly good tractor for a tin of coffee, but it was rather a large souvenir to take home, and anyway, by the rules, it had to go back to the Russians. Meanwhile, in order that aircraft could land and rescue them, they organized parties to clear the bombs the Germans had left upon the runways. There were three especially unpleasant-looking specimens, wired to an electric device for exploding them, which the Germans had evidently not had time to use before clearing out. Volunteers of the incredibly courageous kind who always seem to be found in any British force went out to them and started tinkering. The rest kept well out of range and piously hoped for the best. The expected explosions did not happen, however. After a considerable time the volunteers nonchalantly returned, carrying the bomb fuses, and with the information that the rest of the bombs littering the airfield were quite safe and could be moved away.

The boys therefore moved them, dragging them to an old pit by tractor and then rolling them over the edge. Often they fell on to each other from a considerable height, and Kemp, who was one of the clearing-up party, admits that on such occasions there was a general scramble of people sticking their fingers in their ears and running hard, not that that precaution would have been a bit of use if the entire contents of the pit had decided to go up. However, it never did.

The runways were clear by the evening of May 9th and at 11 am on the following morning two American Flying Fortresses cruised round the airfield and then made a perfect landing on the runway. Even after they had rolled to a standstill the RAF boys saw, appreciatively, that the American crews were standing by their guns, obviously taking no chances with anybody. They also saw that this made a considerable impression upon the Russians.

Next day the evacuation started, with smart American efficiency. One Fortress remained on the aerodrome, acting as a ground control for the other aircraft that came in to pick up and carry away the bands of prisoners who marched up from the camp in orderly parties. Kemp, himself, was on the last aircraft to leave, and their start was somewhat exciting. The American pilot admitted that he was nervous. He was a totally war-trained man and he had never carried a human cargo before, only bombs. His confidence was not increased when he tested the flaps, only to find when he did so that petrol poured out for some reason. However, a ground engineer had a look at things and announced that 'he thought everything would be OK'.

The RAF passengers decided they thought so too.

They wanted to get away from Barth and back to England, and their prevailing mood indicated that they would have been prepared to fly Englandwards in any aircraft, even if it had only one wing.

Therefore, the pilot decided to chance it and took the air. Fortunately, the chance came off. Up in the forward compartment of the aircraft the navigator, an understanding soul, pleased Kemp highly by letting him map-read their course all the way back to Ford airfield, Sussex. On the way the obliging pilot circled the city of Hamburg, just to show the boys and their comrades what a fine mess they had made of it throughout the war.

Sergeant Kemp got down on to British soil at Ford at three o'clock in the afternoon of May 14th, 1945, and walked into his home at three o'clock in the afternoon two days later. He is now a civil servant, happily married and the father of two young daughters. If you meet him any morning in the district of Addington, Surrey, on his daily journey to his Civil Service job, you will naturally find him very much like everybody else for the very good reason that he cannot imagine himself to be 'much different from any other bloke'.

12

CHUTE OPEN—INSIDE THE AIRCRAFT

THE sky over Hamburg in January 1942 was apt to be a lively place. On the night of the 16th of that month the crew of a Stirling aircraft of No3 Group, Bomber Command, met with a very hot reception indeed from the powerful ground defences. Every available piece of local scrap iron which could be propelled by explosive means, together with an assortment of highly inflammable chemicals, was industriously being pumped up from the ground all around them.

The Stirling crew returned the compliment according to the highest traditions of the Royal Air Force by dropping their bomb load as squarely on the target as the bomb-aimer and the pilot could contrive. Then the big aircraft shuddered as a direct hit carried away the starboard inner propeller.

Shortly afterwards the behaviour of the dashboard gauges showed that more than one of the fuel tanks had been holed, so that the petrol was pouring out fast. As the aircraft turned on its homeward course heavy cloud stretched as far as could be seen ahead. Every man on board wondered how far they would get before the inevitable happened.

Would it be a case of jumping before they got clear of enemy-occupied territory, or would they have to ditch the machine in the winter wastes of the North Sea? The night was freezing cold; there was no telling whether the cloud mass reached right down to the earth's surface; so that neither prospect was inviting.

As the long trip dragged on everybody realized that the skipper was doing a nice job. Although he had only three good engines, he nursed the aircraft along carefully, using the fuel from the leaking tanks first and running his remaining engines at the best economical settings. At the same time he shrewdly allowed the big machine a small but constant loss of height in order to get every last yard out of the power available.

At last they knew they had crossed the continental coast and were over the North Sea. To the crew of any aircraft suffering 'trouble' this part of the journey home always seemed an eternity. The men were all grimly tensed bundles of nerves. They said little. They listened to the engines' beat, tried to think of other things, and went on waiting for the faltering note that would mean that the worst had happened.

At last, through a small break in the cloud, they saw that they had passed over the English coast, some miles off course, but still going fairly strong. With nervous tension relaxed, a wave of cheerfulness seemed to pass down the machine. The crew eased themselves in their positions and there was talk and some laughter.

"Do you reckon we can make it?" asked the co-pilot, Flying Officer Baker.

The skipper shrugged. "See that everyone's got a pack on and get them forward," he said. "However far we manage to go, we dare not try to scrape down through ten-tenths cloud. You heard the engineer? We're nearly dry, and the engines may cut at any moment."

As he spoke he was turning the aircraft on the correct course for base, although Baker knew he could never reach it. During the next five minutes, which Baker admits felt nearer five years, the crew got ready and lined up. Then the first engine cut. Almost immediately the remaining two ceased running and the propeller blades became visible, spun for a short time, and then jerkily came to a standstill.

Briefly the skipper gave the order to bale out, his voice sounding unnaturally clear in the sudden silence. This became even more noticeable by reason of the whispering whine of the air outside as he put the big aircraft into a controlled dive.

Baker, as was his duty, stood by and watched the five members of the crew drop away through the escape hatch and instantly disappear in the clear moonlight above the vast carpet of cloud. Then he climbed back up beside the skipper and made his report.

"Everybody away," he said. "Are you all right? Shall I go now?"

The skipper nodded briefly. "Hoppit," he said, "and don't waste time."

The order of abandoning aircraft is one of the strongest regulations in the 'Book' of the Royal Air Force. Only after his entire crew has gone does the skipper finally relinquish control and take to his parachute. Baker therefore obediently jumped down between the two pilots' seats to get clear as soon as possible in order to give his captain every chance. But as he did so the rip-cord of his parachute caught on some projection. What it was he never knew, but the immediate result was that his parachute pack opened, and in the fierce draught from the escape hatch the silken folds of the canopy bellied out behind him and blew *inside* the aircraft.

In giving me his report later, Baker admitted he was more terrified at that moment than he had ever been in the whole of his Air Force career. He knew in that moment that the parachute was probably tearing and ripping itself against the mass of awkward angles, handles and objects with which the interior of any aircraft fuselage is crowded. His hopes of using it as a support in the air, even if he managed to get it clear, could be counted as practically nil. Yet his duty was plain and he acted promptly.

Grabbing the shroud lines in his hands, he wrenched himself up between the seats again and shouted out what had happened.

"Don't wait until I've got the damned thing clear," he yelled. "You can get past these lines. Come on, get away!"

The skipper, however, showed himself to be precisely and exactly what the captain of a Royal Air Force machine should be. His reply was typical.

"Don't be a bloody fool," he said. "Get down and get that thing untangled. Shove it out of the escape hatch. You've still got a chance. If you can't go, I can't . . ."

Baker scrambled down again. What sort of time was left he couldn't tell. When the engines had first cut and the crew had gone away he had marked the altimeter at 6000 feet. How long had passed since then he did not know, but he realized that the aircraft had been rapidly losing height.

Meanwhile, the problem before him was complicated. If he dived straight out of the escape hatch the chances were about a million to one that his parachute would not follow him. If it did, it would merely be a few wisps of ripped and torn silk which would be less support on his journey towards the earth than a girl-friend's sunshade. On the other hand, if he sat on the hatch laboriously gathering up the billowing folds of the canopy from inside the machine, and pushed them out, it was a thousand to one that they would merely entangle themselves around the tail of the aircraft. Nevertheless, the second alternative was obviously the better. Baker therefore scrambled down to the hatch, sat on the edge with his legs dangling over, and gathered his rigging lines, hand over hand, as quickly as he dared, wondering how many tears had developed. As he worked he could feel the whole fabric of the parachute thrashing on the bottom of the fuselage in the incoming draught. Then, as he paid out bunches of the fabric, the force of the wind outside made it jerk violently in its grasp.

Soon he found he could hardly hold against this wrenching pull. The part of the parachute outside the aircraft was pulling itself out of his hands, with part still inside the aircraft. He wondered wildly what he could do. The question was answered before he had time to work it out.

The answer came in the form of a thudding crack over the head dealt him by the edge of the escape hatch. The outside part of the parachute had completely taken charge and dragged him bodily out of the machine. He was three parts dazed, but when his senses cleared he realized he was floating in cloud with the parachute somewhere up above his head in the blackness. Perhaps it is natural that Baker's first instinct was a surge of thankfulness that he was still alive. From the comforting feel of his weight in the web harness, he knew that he was not falling freely. The parachute was sufficiently intact to be giving him support, although he had no means of knowing just how much. His second thoughts were for the aircraft he had left, and for his skipper. But although he listened carefully he could hear nothing, which was not surprising, since the aircraft was without motive power. Otherwise, as most people who have tried it know, parachuting through cloud at night restricts your range of vision pretty well to the end of your nose.

Quite soon, however, there was a difference in the weaving void below him which was difficult to make out in detail, but he knew it meant that he was approaching the ground. He gripped the rigging lines, tensed himself and strained his eyes fiercely. Still nothing showed. Then suddenly he saw a tree, and landed with heavy force, smashing through the thin ice of a shallow, frozen pond.

Awkwardly, in the manner of a hooked fish, he rolled and plunged while his parachute dragged him about twenty yards clear of the pond before it lodged in a bush and collapsed. He staggered very shakily to his feet, released his harness and tried to get his bearings. He found the darkness almost as intense as it had been during his journey down through the cloud. He set out to try to take a straight path—in what direction he had no idea—and for the next hour stumbled in vague circles until at last a cottage loomed up in front of him. Subsequently he found that it was less than a hundred yards from the point at which he had landed.

Not unnaturally, Baker was almost royally entertained by the good folk who lived in the cottage, directly he had knocked at the door and made his presence known. The nearest Royal Air Force station was contacted by telephone and he was given the glad news that all the rest of his crew had landed safely and were being cared for. Of the aircraft and the captain, however, he got no word until he had a night's sleep, when he was given the best and most amusing news of all.

The captain, by a mixture of miraculous good luck and first-class skill, had managed to land the aircraft in the darkness. The landing, as might be expected, had been spectacular. The big aircraft dug its nose into the ground, reared tail-up and then almost disintegrated upside-down. After which, when he could think clearly, the skipper found himself hanging head downwards in his harness. All who have tried it know there is one little difficulty about getting out of a safety harness when in an inverted position. This is to avoid dropping several feet on to one's head, thereby breaking one's neck, directly the release is effected. Nevertheless, the skipper managed it. After which, like Baker, he wandered in circles around the crash shouting and whistling, but unable to find any form of human habitation in the darkness.

Therefore, with commendable good sense, he returned to the crash, climbed into what was left of the fuselage, collected seat cushions and anything else he could find, and calmly settled himself to sleep. The crew of a roving tender from the nearest Air Force station found him in the clear light of day, woke him up and carried him off to a good breakfast, no worse for his night's adventure.

. . . . .

A little over seven months later, on August 24th, 1942, Baker made his second parachute descent of the war. On this occasion he himself was captain of the aircraft and the upshot of the whole incident was that he walked the best part of the way home. It was rather a long walk—but of that more later.

The main point of interest about that summer night was its beauty. The sky was absolutely clear as Baker's bomber aircraft, having completed a mission, crossed the border between Germany and Belgium on its course back to base. High above, the full moon hung like a great silver ball spreading its soft radiance over the sleeping world . . . and the crew hated every square inch of it. This was because a full moon in a clear sky is just about the most dangerous thing that any bomber crew can encounter. It makes their aircraft a silhouetted dead-duck target for any fighters approaching from below. Moreover, it is almost impossible for the aircraft gunners to pick out the small shape of a fighter rising from the green-grey expanse of the ground below until it has got perilously close. Baker therefore was taking his crew home with 'the wicks turned fully up', with everybody tense, and the gunners alert for trouble.

When trouble came none of them actually saw the aircraft which launched it. With a nice, clear target in his sights the pilot of a Me110 must have enjoyed himself as he came up for his first attack from below and dead behind. Even so, he seems to have been a little over-confident, for his first burst did no more than put the rear gun-turret out of action, produce a small fire, and an equally warm stream of remarks from the flight engineer, who jumped violently and winced over a wounded arm.

Baker, at the controls, immediately flung the aircraft into evasive action, but within his heart of hearts he knew that he hadn't a hope. Once again the Messerschmitt came into the attack, and once again the big bomber shuddered as a burst of cannon shells smashed into the starboard wing-tanks, setting up a blaze of fuel which whipped back in the slip-stream.

As captain, Baker now had to make a decision. It was obvious they would have to abandon aircraft, but it would be best for all concerned if they could get as near home as possible before doing so. Meanwhile, the fire was gaining, so he had to decide how long the wing structure would stand up to the terrific heat before it finally collapsed and put the aircraft into a spin from which it might be impossible for anybody to get clear.

However, the only thing to be thankful for was that the Messerschmitt pilot had sheered off, obviously satisfied now that his 'kill' was burning.

For about five minutes Baker kept on course until he felt that the wing could not possibly stand up to the strain much longer. He gave the order to abandon ship but, to his horror, discovered that the intercom had failed, and it was therefore impossible to communicate with his crew.

In that moment of helplessness Baker sat rigid . . . and sweated. The fire was gaining and he knew that at any minute the wing might collapse. The lives of his comrades hung upon his ordering them away, but there was no way of passing the order. He wondered wildly what the hell to do—and then with the miraculous inconsequence which is part and parcel of aircraft in war—the intercom suddenly 'came on' again. Baker gasped and shouted his order.

"Bale out, chaps," he yelled. "Jump, everybody. Make it snappy. Get away as fast as you can."

Those who believe in Fate or Providence will place their own interpretation on the fact that the intercom remained live just long enough for that order to be given. As he spoke the last word, Baker realized that the thing had crackled and gone dead again.

He had no time, however, to relax even in this moment of relief. He put 'George', his automatic pilot, into action, and as his crew came tumbling forward to go out through the escape hatch, he unbuckled his safety harness and heaved himself out of his seat. Then he went aft along the fuselage to make a final check and satisfy himself that all of them had got away.

By this time the fire was just starting to eat its way into the fuselage, so Baker hurried back forward again and took a brief glance at the altimeter, which registered 12000 feet, before he went to the escape hatch and rolled himself headlong into the night. For the next few moments he rolled over and over, the sky gyrating about him before he was jerked upright by the opening of his parachute canopy. In his own words : "At some moment unknown to me I had pulled the rip-cord, but what I had done with it I never afterwards knew. When I found myself swinging safely on the open parachute the ring was no longer in my hand. I think in that moment all I felt was regret that this souvenir was lost.

"Above me was my parachute billowing gently and singing softly in the still night air. Below was the silvery landscapes, trees, rivers, fields and houses, everything I had seen so often from the aircraft, but now its beauty enhanced by the utter stillness. As I seemed to hang unmoving above it all I tried to turn myself this way and that to see what had happened to the others who had left the aircraft. But I only spotted one parachute far away below me and I could only hope that the rest of the chaps had landed safely. Then the thought suddenly came to me that very soon my parents would receive that grim telegram : 'The Air Ministry regrets . . .' I knew what a multitude of fears that terse announcement of 'missing' could carry to parents and what unpleasant visions it might cause. Yet there was I, enjoying the incomparable beauty of an August night over Belgium, and, in one sense, thoroughly enjoying it."

Baker's descent took a long time since he had baled out at considerable height. He saw the abandoned aircraft crash and realized that he was going to land quite close to it. Indeed he actually landed so close that he could make out the figures of the local inhabitants around the wreck and heard their excited voices as they talked and called out to each other. Apparently, however, they did not think of looking up above them, and it seems certain that none of them saw him as he drifted down not far away and settled into the trees of a pine-wood.

He tried to spill his parachute in order to avoid the wood, but could not manage it. Therefore he held his feet tight together and shut his eyes just before he felt himself breaking the small outer branches. With a fairly heavy thud, he found himself rolling over on the pine-needle floor in the middle of the trees, and staggered to his feet, virtually unhurt.

Baker scraped a hole for his parachute in the pine-needles and made sure that it was well hidden. Subsequently, he found that the spot he had landed on was about 20 miles south-west of Brussels. Meanwhile, since it was his object to evade capture, he set off at a brisk pace to put as much distance between himself and the crashed aircraft as possible.

In an earlier part of this story I mentioned that he went for rather a long walk. The distance, in actual fact, was from that spot near Brussels to Gibraltar. He managed it in less than eight weeks, and then got himself aboard a boat for home.

It is typical of him that when I checked the details of his story he said, "I say, old boy, must you use my name? After all, it's the least important part . . . and all that happened to me might have happened to anybody!"

13

WITH HIS PARACHUTE UNDERNEATH HIS ARM

RONALD HAROLD GRANTHAM is one of those cheerful, easy-going people who take the dangers of war and the normalities of peace just as they come without bothering much about either. In September 1941, when he was nineteen years old, he left the world of auctioneering for the Royal Navy and endured the usual AB's three months' preliminary training with as good a grace as the rest. Towards the end of this time he attended a lecture on the work of the Fleet Air Arm, became fascinated by the idea and volunteered for flying duties forthwith.

He was one of about twenty who did so. Of these, five were selected after medical examination for the wireless-operator-flying course. Two of them passed, Grantham being one.

By July 1943, Grantham found himself with 771 Squadron (Fleet Requirements Unit) in the Scapa Flow area with the rank of Acting Leading Airman. He liked flying, enjoyed the life and as a wireless operator his skill was rated all it should be by superiors, including Sub-Lieutenant Smith, with whom on the morning of the 27th of that month he was ordered to fly over ships in the Flow on a predictor control test.

Tests of this kind are made to check the accuracy of anti-aircraft gun predictors, mechanisms which point the gun so that the shell will reach a certain spot in the sky at the same time as its aircraft target. For Grantham and Sub-Lieutenant Smith, however, this exercise was not quite so alarming as it might sound. No actual shells were fired at them, since predictors can be checked for accuracy without such spectacular fun-and-games.

All that is needed is for an aircraft to make a number of runs at different exact heights which have previously been agreed with the predictor crews. Indeed, Grantham took the exercise as a normal matter of everyday life. Once his pilot had climbed the Defiant aircraft in which they were flying to 5000 feet, he settled down in his rear cockpit to read a periodical entitled the *Hotspur*, which for a modest price provides tales of high adventure and derring-do, a form of reading matter which pleasantly relieved his mind from the tedium of war.

Since the Defiant was being used for predictor exercises, the guns had been taken out together with the swivel turret. In place of the latter was a sliding hood over Grantham's cockpit, in which he sat facing rearwards behind the pilot. This suited him down to the ground. He was able to continue his reading with only occasional attention to his wireless set, while Smith, in front, did the work of keeping the aircraft carefully at the agreed levels.

It was a pleasant spring morning, the job for all concerned was an easy one and Grantham was able to give an almost undivided attention to the adventurous people in the pages of the *Hotspur* who were always doing such remarkably dangerous things. Then he heard his pilot over the intercom. He was slightly startled, for the pilot's voice ordered him to prepare to bale out. At the same time he realized that the engine had cut entirely and, in spite of Smith's efforts, was showing no signs of getting going again.

Grantham dutifully dropped the *Hotspur* on the floor of the aircraft and gave full attention to his wireless gear. He rattled out a succession of 'Mayday' signals appropriate to the situation. But then, he tells me, he realized that nothing useful was happening because at that moment one of the ships below started to send powerful signals to another aircraft in the area. Somewhat feverishly he waited for a chance to get through and send the signal again, but the ship was loquacious and did not give him a chance. While this was happening he heard Smith's voice again through the intercom ordering him to clap on his parachute and dive over the side as soon as possible.

Even so, he still thought it was his duty to make sure the 'Mayday' signal went out. Therefore he fiddled feverishly with the set and tried again to make contact, but Smith's order came once more, and this time there was an edge to his voice that could not be disregarded.

Grantham therefore gave up his efforts, grabbed his parachute from the rack where he kept it at the side of the cockpit and put it on. At the same time he tried to get the straps of the dinghy pack on which he was sitting fixed on each side, but, with the lunatic stubbornness such things can have when they are most needed, the second clip eluded his fingers after the first was fastened. Meanwhile, time was pressing and the aircraft was rapidly losing height. Since he was a good swimmer, he decided that, dinghy or no dinghy, he had better take his chance.

Having slammed the cockpit canopy back, he heaved to his feet and leaned out. The sea looked a long way down, and Grantham was vividly conscious of the thought: 'I may be dead in five minutes' time from now.'

One second later he had reason to think he was going to be dead even more quickly, for as he leaned over the side of the cockpit, the slip-stream caught his parachute pack, so that it shot away from him with the upper harness attached.

The parachute was of the detachable type which clips on the wearer's chest, the harness shoulder-straps being looped down and secured with twine which will break with a fairly easy pull. The force of the slip-stream snapped the twine so that the pack broke free and was waving in the air at right angles to him, about a yard away.

Grantham frantically hauled it back by one of the shoulder-straps. Since time was pressing he rammed it under his arm. Then he tumbled headlong out of the machine.

It did not pass through his mind to consider what any hero of the *Hotspur* pages might have done in the same situation, but he admits that his performance lacked a certain grace. In his plunge out, one of his feet caught against something. He was held, wriggling frantically until he could get his other foot against the side of the fuselage, after which he gave a terrific heave—and broke free.

Then, as he somersaulted down the sky, he waited for the expected, comforting jerk of the parachute opening above his head. The jerk didn't come. He looked above his head and saw nothing but the bright blue sky. No sign of a parachute canopy at all.

Something made him look down, and then for a second he was so flabbergasted that he could not move. He saw that he was still holding his closed parachute pack under his arm, like a parcel.

Grantham achieved movement with suddenness. He hurled the pack away from him just as urgently as he had hauled it in a few moments beforehand, at the same time yanking at the release-ring. With a vast relief he saw it bursting open and the canopy streaming and unfolding out in the draught of his fall. As it finally jerked open and he swung on the shroudlines, Grantham breathed deeply, cursed himself with considerable fluency, and then inflated his Mae West. After which, as the water seemed to be coming close, he rehearsed release-drill.

As he did so, he saw a trawler pull out of a line of shipping below and take a course roughly in the direction where he might be expected to meet the waves. This cheered him for a few minutes, until the trawler turned back and went into line again. Then, just when he least expected it, the water came up and hit him with a flop. As he floundered beneath the surface, he instinctively turned the safety-swivel of the harness on his chest. Grantham thereafter explored the depths of Scapa Flow and found them uninviting. His inflated Mae West corked him back up to the surface before he could swallow a dangerous gallonage. Then, as he trod water, getting his breath back, he saw that the harness and parachute shrouds were still attached to him, caught around his left boot. The parachute, still inflated on the surface, was pulling him along with the direction of the wind. So he decided to stay with it for a while.

This method of travel ceased to have its appeal after a while. The parachute began buckling and sinking and the shrouds started tangling round him. Therefore he at last got himself free of the whole thing and managed to kick off his boots as good measure.

Grantham swam for about the next twenty minutes, only occasionally seeing shipping as he floated on the crest of wave-tops. To his relief, a destroyer appeared, pitching and plunging towards him, with a boat swung out ready for launching at the davits. He made out the destroyer's name, *Matchless*, and later decided that it was very suitable. The lowered boat made for his parachute and spent some time picking it out of the water, the crew taking not the slightest notice of his shouts. Then it went further away and stopped again to pick up one of his boots which was still floating. Grantham's plaintive cries became tinged with crossness. He waved his arms and yelled: "Here . . . *here* . . . You silly bastards, I'm not *there*; I'm *here* . . ."

Evidently the boat's crew at last heard something familiar. They turned in his direction, came alongside and hauled him out. But they were evidently determined not to be put in the wrong by anybody that morning. On their way back to the parent ship they turned aside again and picked up his other boot.

After a hot bath in the Petty Officers' Mess and a generous allowance of rum, examination showed that Grantham was none the worse for his adventure. He was generously provided with a pair of grey flannel slacks and a submarine-type white sweater while his clothes and boots were dried in the engine-room. Some time later his helmet, overalls, Mae West and flying-boots were restored to him rolled up in his parachute, and he was dropped off on to a drifter which carried him away and landed him at Stromness.

Having donned his boots and left the rest of his bundle with a watchman, he set off to telephone his home station with a request for transport. After which he lounged about the town still in the sweater and flannels, looking idly in shop windows while he waited for it to turn up.

Suddenly he noticed in the reflection of a window front two burly figures looming up behind him. He turned about and found himself facing two military policemen, who solemnly demanded his means of identification.

Grantham explained that he had parachuted out of an aeroplane and had been rescued and put ashore. The policemen were unimpressed. They asked why he wasn't carrying any flying gear. When he began, laboriously, to explain details they stolidly closed in at his sides and marched him off under close arrest to military headquarters. There it took another half-hour of solemnly farcical cross-questioning and of telephone calls to his home unit before the military finally decided that perhaps he wasn't a spy, and allowed him to go off home in the transport which had turned up to fetch him.

Back at the aerodrome, however, he met his pilot, who stared at him and inquired: "Well, what on earth happened to *you*? I thought you hadn't been able to get out for some reason, so I decided to try a landing. I managed to get away with it, but the crate's a total write-off."

Grantham was demobilized late in 1945 as a full Petty Officer. A year before that he married and now has 'three' children; two girls, and one Ford Eight (1938 vintage) with which he tinkers lovingly in his spare time.

Apart from all of which, he is still the same cheerful, happy-go-lucky creature, and takes life just as it comes.

He is still a member of the Fleet Air Arm Reserve, having passed his air fitness test again two years ago. He is also a very enthusiastic member of the Telegraphist Airgunners' Association (at their Manchester branch), which, he asks me to say, is always keen to regain touch with any 'ex-Tags' of the Fleet Air Arm.

All letters, please, to Secretary Dickie Davis at 66 Barrington Road, Bexley Heath, Kent.

14

'THE INCENDIARY LOAD'S ALIGHT——'

MR A. R. MANSFORD went for a walking tour through south-west Europe in the spring and summer of 1943. His many friends today may find this a little surprising, for Mr Mansford is not fond of walking. He prefers to spend his spare time at home with his wife and three children. He started flying at the age of nineteen, celebrating his twenty-first birthday seven days after returning from the trip detailed here.

He travelled to eastern France by air, and took a stroll from there clear through to Gibraltar, from which point he was fortunate enough to get a boat home to England. The trip took him just about six months in all and the reasons for it are as follows.

On the night of March 8th–9th, 1943, Mansford was a Sergeant (he later became a Flight Lieutenant) in 102 Squadron stationed at Pocklington in Yorkshire. He also occupied the responsible position of bomb-aimer in an all-sergeant crew of a Halifax Mk1 bomber aircraft detailed to carry a full load of incendiary bombs to the city of Nuremburg in Germany.

Since Nuremburg was the place which spawned the Nazi Party, Bomber Command of the RAF took a special pleasure in paying it little visits. The visit scheduled on this occasion was made up of a party of 600 aircraft carrying both incendiary and high explosives. But then Bomber Command never forgot Herr Hitler's announcement that his patience was exhausted, and felt it only polite to show him that theirs was not.

Sergeant Mansford and his friends got away to a normal and uneventful take-off and climbed steadily as they crossed the English coast and droned their way high above Occupied France. The night was pitch dark and there was no moon. Moonlight makes any bomber a nice, big, shiny target, while the smaller, faster fighting aircraft, if they keep at a lower level, are extremely difficult to spot owing to the fact that they 'fade in' to the dark relief map of the ground below, and can nearly always make an unexpected attack.

However, as most people have discovered, nothing is perfect. A dark, moonless night is as dangerous to a bomber crew as a night of full moon if they do get themselves spotted by an enemy fighter. If they can't see him they have no means of hearing him. The first hint they are likely to get of his presence is a stream of cannon shells bashing into their aircraft. Even then those members of the crew who don't happen to be killed or badly wounded can't see anything to fire back at.

This was precisely what happened to the Halifax in which Sergeant Mansford was sitting in his usual position above his bomb-aiming gadgetry, almost directly above the escape hatch in the nose of the aircraft. Up to that point all had gone well. The aircraft was dead on course, the engines were running sweetly and the forest of the Argonne was a faint, indeterminate patch sliding by in the darkness below. Even so, every member of the crew were keeping a specially bright look-out, especially the rear-gunner. When it came to action he knew he could give any attacking fighter a blasting-hot reception, if he saw it first. If he didn't, he was usually dead before he could fire his guns, anyway.

On this occasion the rear-gunner was lucky. The business of seeing a black-painted fighter against a background of that kind was as easy as spotting a black cat in a coal cellar without a light. The gunner had not the faintest idea that an enemy was within miles of him when a livid line of tracers suddenly flared out of the darkness behind the aircraft. The burst of cannon shells missed his gun-turret, although they passed hideously close. He grabbed for his triggers, thankful that the surprise attacker's first shot had been just off-aim. He was still alive, and had something to fire back at—the focal point of the tracer stream.

But even as he sent a burst blazing back in return, he found himself in the middle of a furnace. It was a very lively furnace because the attacker's first burst of cannon shells, although they had missed the rear gun-turret, had gone straight into the aircraft bomb-bays, which were loaded with incendiaries.

The immediate result will, I think, be clear enough to the normal imagination. The incendiary load went up, and in the next few seconds the aircraft, without exaggeration, was just an enormous torch of flame racing across the sky as its engines still pulled it along. Meanwhile, the rear-gunner and the rest of the crew heard their pilot shouting over the intercom : "Bale out. Jump, everybody. Don't waste time. Get out. We've had it, chums."

Mansford, in the nose of the machine, set about obeying the order. He knew his first duty was to wrench open the forward escape hatch and then clear his navigator of certain gear before jumping himself. But as he started he was privately convinced that the petrol tanks would explode in the roaring blaze before he could finish. At this moment the escape hatch decided to stick. No matter how he wrenched and tore at it, the hatch wouldn't budge.

During this sudden check in the regulation proceedings for escape, the navigator managed to clear himself. He joined Mansford at the hatch and added his efforts with some urgency. Then Mansford found himself getting 'all thumbs'. He fell against the hatch when he should have been pulling. He realized very abruptly that this was because he was lying head-down at a sharp angle because the aircraft had gone into a steep dive. He had the sensation of standing on his head as he braced his elbows and pulled again as best he could manage. Perversely, the hatch decided to come open at that moment with a sudden thud and inrushing gale from the speed of the dive. Mansford recovered himself, saw that the navigator was shouting something and gesturing for him to get out. It was not a moment in which to stand upon ceremony. He took a headlong dive through the hole, and in an instant passed from a blistering, stinking uproar of fire and confusion into almost unearthly silence and the clear sweetness of the night air.

It was an amazing, unreal change that he remembers vividly even to this day. Just below him and some distance away he saw the flaming torch which had been the Halifax bomber diving down the sky like a nightmare comet, throwing off sparks and blazing fragments of fabric which seemed to hang still in its wake. He wrenched at the ring of his parachute, but in that vast gulf of darkness he had no sensation of falling until suddenly he felt a violent jerk on his body harness and heard the thudding crack of the canopy opening somewhere above his head. What had happened to the rest of the crew—whether the navigator had come out after him—he had no idea. The burning wreck did not give enough light for him to spot any other parachute in the sky. Moreover, it was dwindling as it dived with continually increasing speed on its last journey earthwards. By then Mansford guessed that the wings had probably gone, and what remained was only a heavy airframe weighted with engines and having no supporting surfaces at all. At last it went in. Far below he saw it dissolve into a splashing explosion, a vivid yellow burst of flame, and then almost immediately it began to shrivel and die out. Some time before he began to approach the ground, swinging gently beneath his parachute, the fire had died away altogether and he could not tell where in the vague darkness it had once been.

Many months were to pass before he had the good news that all the crew, including the pilot, had managed to bale out in time and had survived the ordeal. Meanwhile, he realized that the ground was coming up to meet him fast, although he could make out no actual detail. Fearing trees, he clapped his feet together, hung on to his main harness supports and tried to judge his landing in accordance with the instruction book. At that moment something hit him and he realized he was turning head over heels in a grass field. When Mansford managed to get to his feet and cast off his harness, his head was swimming and he had a ripe assortment of bumps and abrasions.

The vague silhouettes of houses showed some distance away and he guessed that he was probably on the edge of a village. He set to work to bury his parachute in a hedge, and although he stopped to listen, heard no sound of life anywhere at all. He wondered if the villagers had gone out to the now extinct crash, but decided that they were more likely to be in their cellars, since they must have had a raid warning, and thought that the crashing aircraft was a bomb.

As to his position, he only knew that the navigator had checked them as just passing over the forest of Argonne when they were attacked and set on fire. Calculating roughly, he reckoned the time to be about 10.30 pm, not a pleasant hour to find oneself alone in enemy-occupied country, with one's home and friends hundreds of miles away, and with the width of the North Sea between.

Mansford pulled himself together, climbed the hedge into a country lane and walked along until he found the village. No lights were showing; all was still and everyone in the place seemed to be asleep. Still, the spring night was cold and he was feeling pretty tuckered up. He looked at the cottages, chose one at random, went up to the front door and knocked. There was a movement from inside and then the door opened, dazzling his eyes with the unaccustomed light from within. He could make out no detail of the man who had answered his summons and was about to make use of what French he had in a polite request for something to eat and somewhere to rest. The shadowy man reached out at once, took his arm and pulled him inside the house, shutting the door firmly. It was Mansford's lucky night, in one respect. In a German-occupied village he had blindly chosen the house of the most courageous and resourceful member of the local Resistance. Since he had come, virtually, from the Sergeants' Mess at Pocklington in a matter of hours, and had not yet encountered a single German, it was difficult for Mansford to grasp the full meaning of his own good luck. He had come from friends to friends. The Resistance man and his family received him as an honoured guest, made sure he had no serious wounds, fed him, warmed him and gave him a comfortable bed. In the days that followed they found him a complete outfit of clothes so that he could pass as a labourer, also the necessary forged papers. And they helped him brush up his French.

When he announced himself fit enough, they helped him start out on the little walking tour he had planned. But from first to last they flatly refused to take a centime of the 2000 francs of escape-money which he had with him. By the passing of messages, his first friend and the rest of the Resistance group arranged that he went from 'hand to hand' from the Argonne forest across France to the Spanish border. From there he walked straight across Spain to Gibraltar, where he got his boat for home.

I cannot give too much space to this part of his story, but I have to record that, in the course of being passed from one pocket of Resistance to another during his journey over France, he had a bad fall. At first he thought he had broken both his right arm and his right leg, but these injuries turned out to be 'merely' badly wrenched and torn muscles.

Mansford has never tried to walk on a broken leg, but he was to discover that a torn muscle can't provide much less in the way of pain. Once he found he could walk at all it still hurt like the devil, and for weeks afterwards, whenever he thought his injuries were getting slightly better, back came the pain with unexpected force.

At last, when he was assured that it would be safe for him to get on a train for Paris, he had to change at Epinay. And there, while he was propping up a pillar, waiting for his connection, he recognized his navigator standing on the opposite platform. The navigator, dressed in much the same way as himself, certainly looked the part perfectly and Mansford wondered whether he was doing as well. However, as the station was thick with German troops, the two dared do no more than recognize each other furtively with their eyes. They did not smile, much less wave. Then two trains came in, going in opposite directions, and the two escapees went their different ways.

Later on, when Mansford was being 'passed' across Paris, he met his engineer, who was also being helped by the Resistance people. They had the chance of a talk, but neither of them could give much news of the rest of the crew. Since each had planned different escape routes, and had confidence in his own ideas, they, too, parted after shaking hands and wishing each other luck.

From there Mansford hitched rides on donkey-carts, carrier wagons and any other vehicles he thought might offer a safe ride across France up into the Pyrenees to the town of Froix on the Spanish border. At that period both his leg and his arm were giving him one of their specially bad times, and he was weakened by his privations and the long trek. At Froix his Resistance friends showed their amazing efficiency. By the time he arrived they had gathered a crowd of American, French and other nationalities who were hoping to get across the border. On the day they set out, however, Mansford felt so ill, and could go along so very slowly, that he persuaded the rest of the group to go ahead and leave him to make his own way.

In this he probably had his greatest piece of good luck. Although he crossed soon after the group made their attempt, he never met any of them again or heard anything about them. It seems probable that they either ran into a trap or were seen by the frontier guards and shot down (as was usual), or at best carted away into prison camps. The truth of this is made more than probable by his own experience when he reached the frontier.

He saw the guardhouse, but there was no one in it or anywhere around. He scouted carefully for outpost troops, but the whole area seemed to be deserted. When at last he decided to make the attempt he walked straight over on to Spanish ground and limped down into the first village . . . and no one fired a shot at him in anger.

The obvious inference is that the local guards had just been occupied on other business, and were not expecting a lone fugitive to come creeping through immediately after, as they must have thought, he had seen a large group captured.

Mansford, as I have said, managed to get himself down to Gibraltar, from where he was repatriated to England, arriving home on September 3rd, 1943, the fourth anniversary of the day war broke out.

About that journey there is one small detail I should like to add. When at last he set foot on English soil, Mansford still had in his pockets quite a proportion of the 2000 francs escape-money he had been carrying when he baled out of the Halifax. Since the full total represented only £2 or £3, I consider this to be something of a financial achievement even for a man who is now, I am happy to say, a highly efficient cashier.

15

ODOUR COLOGNE

SERGEANT G. H. 'DIXIE' LEE of 102 Squadron, Royal Air Force, had, and still has, a nice singing voice. He loves light music, especially of the blues type, and since that form of melody is generally approved by RAF personnel, Dixie not only won a nickname, but was much in demand when anyone was around who could agitate a piano. Also, since he was, and still is, a cheerful creature who doesn't believe in letting things get him down, he usually whiled away the time he spent in his rear-gunner's cockpit by bursting into song.

For once in his life, however, Dixie did not feel like warbling sweet strains about the Swanee River when in the gunner's cockpit of a big Halifax which, on April 27th, 1942, was taking off from a Yorkshire airfield with a heavy bomb-load scheduled for the city of Cologne. Seven sergeants including Dixie made up the crew, but none was feeling light-hearted. For Larry Carr, the skipper, had found that the aircraft wouldn't unstick, when he was too far down the runway to do anything about it.

Here I will explain that once you have got an aircraft moving so fast that you can't stop before it reaches the end of the runway, you've 'had it' unless you can make it rise into the air. If the aircraft won't take off, you are going to bash into the hedge at the end, plunge over rough ground and almost inevitably wipe off your undercarriage and roll over and crash. If your petrol tanks are chock-full, as in this case, you will most certainly die in a spectacular cremation. If you have a full bomb-load, the results will be even more awe-inspiring, with the one advantage, of course, that you are unlikely to hear the bang.

One way and another, things had been dicey for the lads of 102 Squadron for some days past. The big Halifax aircraft with which they had been equipped had proved too heavy for their own grass airfield and sank their wheels up to the axles in the mud which had resulted from the April rains. Therefore the aircraft had been moved to the satellite airfield where there was a concrete runway. But even this seemed hair-raisingly short for a bomber of the type, especially when the wind was blowing across it at an angle, as it was on this night.

As a final item to make the picture complete, this was the very first time this crew of seven sergeants had set off on a major operational trip in a Halifax, anyway.

With his engines wide open at full boost, Skipper Larry Carr tried to make the bomber take-off, and saw he was running out of runway fast. It wasn't until disaster seemed absolutely certain that he felt the wheels sluggishly leave the surface. Even so, he had an uncomfortable feeling that they were going to hit the boundary hedge which was racing towards them.

He was right. They did.

With a shudder the big aircraft bashed its undercarriage wheels through the aerodrome hedge, sending up a spectacular shower of broken bushes and twigs in the slip-stream. This interesting display was observed at close quarters by Dixie Lee in his rear gun-turret. He was the first man of the tense crew to break silence since the aircraft had started rolling.

"I don't suppose they *wanted* that hedge, anyway," came his voice over the intercom. "Still, Skipper, I'd rather take a *return* ticket to Cologne if it's all the same to you."

The aircraft kept on level keel and since it had not lurched down and crashed into the ground, Dixie's cheerful loquaciousness can be understood. But he was in the rear of the aircraft, looking back, so he naturally couldn't see what Skipper Carr could see dead in front. The view before the Sergeant was still depressing. Directly ahead were the vast, dark shapes of a group of hangars of the parent airfield which seemed to rise higher than the heavily loaded Halifax was flying. Carr hadn't any hope of making a turn. As the hangars raced nearer and nearer he tensed himself at the controls, feeling quite certain that the aircraft was going to crash straight into the roofs.

But the Halifax just made it. By how many inches he cleared the danger, Carr never knew. At one moment he was sure of death; and at the next the great, black shapes had flicked by without the wheels actually scraping them. Then there was only the broad clear acreage of the Yorkshire Wolds stretched out in front.

Carr relaxed and perspired. Now that the worst was over he was able to offer up thanks for good luck. When he selected 'wheels up' he felt the comforting click as they retracted and locked correctly in place. He found that the aircraft would climb reasonably well and with the altimeter registering comfortably, he flew dead on course for the North Sea and his destined target.

In the rear gun-turret Dixie Lee began crooning a blues. In the navigator's position, Sergeant Ronnie Shoebridge indicated the general relief with a cheerful remark.

"Well," he said, "Cologne may be a stinking target, but the stink will smell nice to me when we've pranged it up and turned for home again."

"Odour Cologne," said someone else. "Listen to the sound of broken glass when we shake up the scent-bottles."

By that time the Halifax was crossing the French coast at about 12000 feet and the moon above was shining, silvery and serene. Dixie noticed that there was hardly anything coming up in the way of flak, and that there were only a few searchlight beams. He didn't care for it and stopped singing to speak to the mid-upper gunner.

"Jimmy, I don't like this much," he said. "They're too quiet down below, and that bloody moon's too damned bright. Better keep your eyes skinned for fighters."

He had hardly finished speaking when a black shape flicked across the moon, and he saw the unmistakable silhouette of a fighter aircraft about 600 yards away.

Jimmy also spotted it. Both yelled "Fighter to starboard, Skipper" at the same time and swung their guns. But Larry Carr at the controls tossed the big Halifax into weaving evasive action at their warning and in a minute or so it seemed that he had shaken the enemy off.

Even so, Dixie felt that it was only a foretaste of plenty of bother to come. The brilliant moonlight conditions were all in favour of any attacker, since the slower-moving bomber aircraft was illuminated almost as clearly as by day, and the vast dim cavern of the sky would give an attacker every chance of making an unexpected pounce. Which was exactly what happened a few minutes later.

Tense, keyed up and straining his eyes, Dixie suddenly saw a Me110 whipping out of the void and diving straight upon them. He yelled a warning to Carr, who again threw the aircraft into a violent weave, but the approaching fighter knew his business. He kept dead on his target, and when he was at about 350 yards both he and Dixie opened fire at each other almost at the same instant.

Amidst the terrific din that filled Dixie's gun-turret he was suddenly half-blinded by a brilliant flash. At the same time he felt a sharp, stabbing pain in one foot. One of the enemy's cannon shells had scored a square hit on the turret, striking his ammunition feed. But the rest of the burst had also scored. A matter of seconds later the whole port-side of the Halifax was a roaring mass of flames which swept back in the slip-stream.

The shaken and wounded Dixie heard Carr shout the order over the intercom for the whole crew to bale out.

At the same time he realized that the aircraft had gone into a headlong dive. Dazedly he groped for his parachute pack, but as he did so he suddenly saw that the German pilot was coming in for the kill.

As was so often the case in actions of the kind, the man in the fighter was over-confident. He flew in, dead close, thinking that he could be in no possible danger from his falling and blazing victim. But Dixie Lee was ready for him. As he closed in, Dixie had his gun-sights dead on and let fly with a burst that poured squarely into the approaching German. The fighter immediately burst into a blaze and spun over, to dive earthwards.

During this time, with the prescience that sometimes comes to a man in fierce emergency, Dixie had heard the navigator and the second-pilot ordered away in their parachutes. He felt the aircraft give a terrific jerk and guessed that the skipper had also gone, leaving the control stick free.

For the second time he groped for his parachute pack, found it and slammed it into his harness clips. But while he was doing so there was an uproar of approaching cannon fire—he thinks it was the first of the two fighters which had returned—and again he grabbed for his guns. This time he could only fire at random and had no idea if he had hit anything. Meanwhile, he knew that the Halifax had been whining down the sky in a dive and he had no idea as to just when it would smash into the ground and obliterate him. The thought came into his mind that he was not going to get out at all, for he found that the hydraulic mechanism which rotated his turret had been shot to pieces. The only way to get out of a Halifax rear gun-turret of that type was to revolve it round and escape through the doors.

Dixie did the only thing possible, and set to work to revolve it by hand, having no idea whether he was at 500 feet, 5000 feet or only 50. At last he got it round far enough so that he could heave up and start forcing himself through the turret doors, but then he found his legs jammed. He plunged and struggled, but somehow his trousers had got caught in the turret mechanism.

As a last resort he decided to pull the release-ring of his parachute, hoping that as it streamed out and cracked open it would forcibly jerk him from where he was held. At which point he found that he had put his parachute on the wrong way round.

Actually, this proved to be such a lucky mistake that it saved his life. His right arm was so jammed that he would not have been able to get at the release-ring had the parachute pack been put on correctly. As it was he found the ring with his left hand, and gave it an almighty wrench. The next thing he knew was a terrific jerk on his body harness, a wrenching pain from his wounded foot, and he was out in the open air.

Almost immediately afterwards, it seemed, two things happened simultaneously. There was a roaring explosion as the aircraft smashed into the ground and, as he swung like a human pendulum on his parachute rigging, Dixie's feet clattered through the twigs of a tree-top. Just what the height was when he finally got out of the blazing Halifax he naturally doesn't know, but at the most it must have been only a few hundred feet from the ground. A second or so later he landed and rolled over in the middle of a field, knocked half-dazed by the thud of meeting the earth. He managed to free himself from his parachute harness and then picked himself up, finding himself not far from the crashed bomber.

Three of that gallant crew of seven died in those few minutes of action. Only Dixie, Larry Carr the skipper, Ronnie Shoebridge the navigator, and Sergeant Ralston, a Canadian, survived.

At that time, of course, Dixie had no idea of what had happened to the others. He got himself to a village and was there befriended by some of the inhabitants. Soon afterwards, however, he found himself in German hands because one of the villagers, a collaborator, had given him away.

Ironically enough, his capture by a party of German soldiers was witnessed by Larry Carr, his skipper, who had also managed to get to the village and had obtained a suit of civilian clothes. Carr was already starting a cross-country bid for escape and until that moment had no idea that Dixie was around. As it was, he could only watch the arrest, powerless to do anything to help. Subsequently, the men of the Underground movement helped him make a clean escape, so that in a matter of weeks he got home.

Dixie Lee spent the rest of the war a prisoner, varying the tedium by making several fruitless attempts at escape.

At last came the end of the fighting and his repatriation. One thing which brought an even greater satisfaction to his homecoming was the news of the quisling who had caused his capture by the Germans. This unpleasant individual, he learnt, had been put on trial shortly afterwards by members of the local Underground movement, sentenced and quietly executed.

16

THE SHIP THAT PASSED BY

THERE is a letter before me dated 16-9-41 with the officially-vague superscription 'Middle East Forces'. I will quote the first paragraph :

> 'My very dear Mother, I reckon that you must have been praying pretty hard for me last Tuesday as a blooming Jerry shot me down into the sea and I am still alive to tell the tale. I cannot give you the whole story or else I might upset the censor. However, I think he'll pass this letter if I tell you just something . . .'

The censor had no qualms in passing the very brief and matter-of-fact details so typical of the average young pilot's letter to his mother. As always in such letters, there is not a single hint of a self-glorification on the part of the writer. It just announced baldly that he and his squadron were unexpectedly attacked by enemy aircraft whilst on fleet patrol over the Mediterranean, and that he had to get out in his parachute and land in the water. Subsequently he was picked up and had to have a couple of days' rest in Tobruk before going back to flying duties. "I didn't like Tobruk much—too much bombing, but that may have been because I was rather tired. Anyway, all I got was a number of minor abrasions, some bruises and a nasty stiff neck. Next thing I have to get is my revenge. Love to all the family and lots to yourself. Your affectionate son, James."

This is what actually happened when Squadron Leader James W. Marsden took his swim in the Mediterranean and subsequently wrote the letter I have quoted, which must have been maddening to his mother in its lack of detail.

Marsden at the time was Commanding Officer of 33 Squadron, RAF. On the day in question the Squadron was detailed to give fighter cover to a convoy about 40 miles out from the coast which was proceeding to Tobruk. They were flying Hurricane aircraft, but although they had parachutes and inflatable Mae Wests, they had not, at that period of the war in that area, yet been provided with collapsible rubber dinghies.

The patrol was much the same as dozens of others the Squadron had carried out, often uneventful but always dangerous for two special reasons. The first was the bright Mediterranean sun, in the glare of which enemy aircraft might at any time be hiding, ready to make an unexpected jump. The other was the fact that although the Hurricane was, in its time, one of the finest fighting aircraft which ever came into service, it was a great deal slower than the Me109s with which the German Middle East Forces were equipped.

Naturally enough, Marsden and his comrades kept their eyes peeled as they went about their double duty of both looking for trouble and trying to be sure that they spotted it in time. The German Luftwaffe was far too fond of 'beating up' convoys and raking them with fire from fighter aircraft, quite apart from bombing attacks by the heavier machines; and 33 Squadron was on duty to discourage this light-hearted practice.

However, as has happened so often before, the glare of an almost tropic sun proved their undoing. Suddenly the attack came. Marsden had a momentary glimpse of a machine he automatically identified as an Me109F, and was about to snap orders to the rest of the Squadron when his controls jerked violently within his hand. A moment later he realized that they had been shot away.

There was a thud as his petrol tank was pierced, and flames began to blast along the fuselage. At the same time he was blinded by oil drenching back from a severed pipe connection, and half-choked by fumes.

Marsden knew that his machine had gone into a screaming dive and there was nothing he could do to right it. He grabbed at the cockpit canopy to wrench it back, but it wouldn't move and he saw that the runners were jammed by the frayed edges of bullet holes which had been shot through it. Just why he himself was alive—and, as far as he could judge, not badly wounded—he had no idea. In any case, with his altimeter showing less than 6000 feet and unwinding fast as the machine plummeted down, he didn't care to waste time in thought.

Somehow, by the frantic strength which a man is so often able to find in moments of fierce emergency, he at last shifted the canopy and wrenched it back far enough so that he could wriggle through. As he did so, he saw that both his hands were covered with blood, but since they were both working for him he didn't pay much attention.

With a mighty kick and a heave he got away over the side, plunging head over heels as he groped for his parachute release-ring and wrenched it hard. There was the usual almighty crack from above, and the breath-taking jerk from his harness, as the faithful parachute filled out and checked his fall. For the next few minutes he hung there, swinging gently, and examining himself for damage.

It was then he realized that the sheet of armour-plate behind the Hurricane pilot's seat had undoubtedly saved his life. The blood on his hands was from bullet grazes, but one of those bullets had smashed his wristwatch to pieces. Apart from that, as far as he could tell, he hadn't got a hole in him. Meanwhile, he could see that he was coming down well ahead of the convoy ploughing its way across the ocean below. So, one way and another, he reckoned he'd come out of the whole thing pretty luckily.

His reckoning was rather premature. Suddenly he heard the drone of an aircraft engine, glanced round apprehensively, and then hunched his shoulders as the unmistakable form of an Me109F came diving down directly at him with its guns blazing. The next few minutes were hectic. Marsden was attacked more than once as he hung helpless on his parachute, a dangling marionette of a target for the excited German pilots. How the spraying bullets missed him he never knew; he could only thank heaven that German marksmanship was far below the efficiency of the equipment they had to hand. In any case, the attacks broke off as suddenly as they had started, and then, as he finally ventured to look round again, he realized a phenomenon quite normal in air fighting.

The sky seemed to be clear. Of either Hurricanes or Me109s there was nothing to be seen. There was only the ocean, the vast, golden bowl of the sunlight . . . and away behind the white wake of the convoy a couple of parachutes going down, and some plumes of smoke coming up from the water where the aircraft had crashed.

Marsden hoped that none of his own comrades was on either of those parachutes. At that time, owing to the danger of submarine attack, no ship dared turn back out of a convoy, and thus risk the safety of the rest. Therefore, those who dropped into the sea after a convoy had gone by had practically no hope of rescue unless it came from some other direction. And there was no sign at all of other shipping.

In this, I regret to say, Marsden's hopes were doomed. Three pilots of 33 Squadron, who were shot down in that action, fell behind the convoy, and were never heard of again.

As he tensed himself to hit the water, and went through the normal drill for casting off his parachute gear, Marsden marked the direction of the convoy carefully. He knew that, at all costs, he must keep himself directly in its path. Then he took his ducking, but when he finally came up to the surface he found that, owing to the waves, he could not see any of the ships at all.

Only for a brief second, when he was carried high, could he make out a drift of smoke, which he knew must come from one of the funnels. So he swam as steadily as he could in that direction. After some time, and when he seemed to get no nearer, he became deadly frightened that he might not keep in the path of the ships at all. He had no means of checking their speed or of knowing whether they ought to be close around him now, or still on their way. Therefore he took the blind chance of undoing his Mae West and throwing it away, so that he could swim faster.

What sort of distance Marsden actually covered it would be impossible to say. From the evidence of those who saw him come down on his parachute, he learned afterwards that he swam for a solid two hours. At last, to his utter relief, as he rose on a wave, he saw the grey form of a ship quite near, and making towards him. What kind of ship it was he neither knew nor cared.

He trod water and waved wildly as it loomed up, towering over him and coming closer and closer. Then Marsden made quite a ghastly discovery; the ship was actually going past him, and it was going fast. He did not know the reason then, but the eyes of those on board were upon his parachute, which they could still see floating a considerable distance off. It was to the parachute that they were making their way in the hopes of picking him up, not realizing that the tiny blob of his head was almost at the side of their own vessel as they went by.

So close was Marsden that he was caught up and tossed in the curving wash from the side. High up on that side, by a nightmare coincidence, he saw the ship's number, the large figures '33', the number of his own Squadron. As he realized the freakishness of this, he also understood that he was in every danger of getting washed into the ship's propellers and cut to pieces. He gave up waving and yelling, and turned over to swim away as fast as he could from the approaching menace.

It was then, if ever, that blind good luck served him to the full. A Norwegian sailor moving about the deck of the ship happened to glance over the side and saw him thrashing through the water. The man did the only thing that could have been done in the circumstances, but a very brave thing it was. He yelled to his comrades and took a flying leap over the side, straight into the water. A few minutes later he was supporting the practically exhausted Marsden. Signals were flashed down the convoy and soon a lifeboat's crew was away, to pick up the castaways and haul them both on board.

I should just like to quote a few more lines from the letter Marsden wrote to his mother, which has already been noted. It expresses rather nicely the mentality of the young fighter pilot of the time, and I think, we shall find, of any time.

> 'Of course I got a terrific reception when I got back to the Squadron. I have just got six more pilots to-day, and some more aeroplanes. Your airgraph letter dated 23rd just received, for which many thanks. Glad you are still comfortable at Canford Cliffs, but the chances of my spending Xmas with you there seem to be rather remote. . . .'

17

KNIFE WITHOUT ANÆSTHETIC

LIEUTENANT WINTON SEXTON's story of his thirtieth mission is probably one of the strangest ever to be brought back by a pilot to the Intelligence Officers of the United States Air Force. In the winter of 1943 the American 12th Bomber Group, equipped with B25 aircraft, was operating from Sicily. Sexton and his comrades were well-seasoned warriors. They had formed the first light bomber group to fight in Africa side by side with the British Eighth Army in Egypt. Now they had made their first big stride along a path which was to take them from Cairo clear through to Naples.

The objective of Sexton's thirtieth mission was a heavily-fortified area on the slopes of Mount Etna. The B25s thundered away down the airstrip, made formation in the clear sunshine, and then took course for target. Soon they were joined by a big formation of Spitfires from a British airfield which was to give them fighter cover.

Throughout the African campaign the Americans had flown with Spitfire cover, and their respect for the British fighter boys was sky high. Sexton admits that he wasn't feeling too spry that morning, and the sight of that perfect formation of small machines gave him very considerable comfort.

Soon he had the information 'crossing enemy lines' over the intercom, and he and his crew put on their helmets. At that period of the war the helmets were their only protection, since flak suits, which were developed later, hadn't become standard equipment. Meanwhile, they had all previously had cause to know that the German gunners were dangerously accurate in this special area. For the time being, however, nothing marred the peace of the early morning. Even Etna seemed to be sleeping as soundly as the rest of the Italian countryside, only a faint haze of smoke hanging above the volcanic crater. As the bomb-aimer began settling down to his instruments, Sexton recalled a feeling of remorse. He said afterwards that it seemed a hell of a time in the morning to be starting a war again. Yet he found himself automatically concentrating on steadying the run as the bomb-aimer got his sights on the target.

Then the quiet earth was stabbed by pin-points of flame, and up came the anti-aircraft shells. Half a dozen of them exploded above and ahead of the American machines but even so the concussion was heavy.

"Dozey stuff," chuckled one of the crew. "Those guys haven't unstuck their eyes yet."

Sexton, steadying the controls of the pitching aircraft, didn't join in the joke. He knew the methods of the German gunners only too well, and he also knew that the first burst had been an extremely good sighting-shot for both height and range. Soon the stuff was coming up all round them; heavy, concentrated, uncomfortably close. Different-coloured smoke was appearing from some of the shell-bursts, and Sexton had already learned that colour-shells could be a German sign calling in fighter attack and notifying their own fighters that, if they came into the party, their gunners would cease fire and leave them to make their kills undisturbed.

Quite obviously, trouble was on the way. The escorting Spitfires evidently expected it too. They broke up their beautiful formation and then closed in round the B25s, taking up strategic positions.

Sexton came up towards the target on his final run, held everything as steady as he could, and then felt the response of the aircraft as the first of the bombs dropped away. The anti-aircraft barrage was as bad as he had ever known, but it gave him something to be thankful for. Evidently no German fighters were in the vicinity yet.

Suddenly the job was over. All the bombs were away and as he turned the big aircraft and headed for home he was satisfied to feel the bomb-doors snap shut, as yet undamaged by enemy fire. Now it was simply a matter of running like fury until they were out of the worst of the ack-ack fire and could look forward to getting back to a decent breakfast.

That breakfast, however, was not on the menu for Sexton or his crew. Just when he thought he was getting the aircraft clear of the fiercest area of shelling, something happened. He had no idea he had been hit, and he didn't actually feel any pain. He was conscious of a heavy sensation—of aching—and in a dazed kind of way realized that he could neither see nor hear. Gradually, things cleared and he found himself staring into his upturned helmet which had fallen between his legs, staring stupidly at a dripping of blood which was going down straight into it. It became obvious that the blood was his own, and he was hunched forward over the controls. With a tremendous effort he wrenched himself upright, to find that his radio-set and sun glasses were gone. He saw a curiously awkward heap in the co-pilot's seat at his side, and realized that it was a dead man.

By now, consciousness and full clarity were coming back to him fast. He glanced out of the right window and saw that the whole right wing of the aircraft was a mass of flame. There was one thing and one thing only to do; to get his crew out, and get out after them. He undid his safety-belt and made to stand up, but his left leg gave way beneath him, and he pitched straight into the navigator's compartment. The fall half-dazed him again and then he found that he was surrounded by smoke and choking fumes. With blood running into his eyes and almost blinding him he groped for the emergency-door release and wrenched it. Nothing happened. At that moment Sexton realized another man was beside him. He heard the bomb-aimer shouting at him to get the door released. He yelled back that it was stuck, and that he couldn't stand up and get a kick at it. The bomb-aimer settled the matter by stamping hard, nearly going headlong out as the thing fell away and then disappeared in the slip-stream outside.

"What about the rest of the boys?" yelled Sexton.

"I know some have gone," answered the bomb-aimer, "but I couldn't see any more. The whole crate's full of smoke."

Sexton gave a nudge and jerked with his thumb. He knew already that the co-pilot was dead without going into any detail. One sight of his huddled figure had been complete evidence of that. Since he couldn't check on the rest of the crew, he had only one duty left, to see that the bomb-aimer went ahead of him. No man in an aircraft that looks like losing a wing at any moment needs a great deal of urging. Directly the man had gone Sexton dragged himself to the hole and got his legs over the edge. The effort jerked him with pain but he set his teeth and dropped out into the hurricane blast.

So awkward was his getaway that he realized during one unpleasant second that he was hard up against the fuselage with the side of his face sliding along the hot aluminium. Then in the usual way of things, the aircraft seemed to disappear entirely. It was gone, together with the smoke, the flames and the uproar, and in the quietude of bright sunshine he had the impression that he was floating.

Since he reckoned he had around 6000 feet in hand, and that he must have left the aircraft at about a couple of hundred miles an hour, Sexton groped for his parachute ring but delayed pulling it for a few seconds. He managed to get an arm up and wipe the blood from his half-blinded eyes, and thereupon saw with something of a shock that he was very much closer to the earth than he would have thought possible in the time. However, in answer to his frantic jerk on the ring, the parachute cracked open above his head and jerked at his harness with comforting effect. At which moment he has the idea that he fainted.

He was only a few hundred feet from the ground, undoubtedly revived by the cold morning air, when he recovered and saw two other parachutes drifting down some distance away. He spotted the blazing aircraft and almost cried in pleasure as he saw yet another parachute open out and inflate in the smoke of its trail down the sky. That meant that at least three of the boys had got clear.

It seemed only a couple of seconds later that he saw the blazing wreck dive headlong into the side of the mountain, the remaining petrol tanks exploding in a vast column of flame and smoke. He realized that all gun-fire had stopped. Far, far away in the distance he saw the sun glinting on the formation of aircraft with which he had been flying a few minutes beforehand. At that sight he felt lost, lonely and wretched. The boys were going home to breakfast. Well out of range of the ack-ack fire, and with the Spitfires still covering them, they would have nothing much to worry about before they landed in the old familiar surroundings. They would probably be tearing open letters from home as they settled down to their coffee and eggs. In the last few seconds of his fall to earth

Sexton saw a small house almost directly below him with a cluster of people standing before it. Since he also saw a flutter of women's skirts, he decided that it was not a German outpost, and therefore he hoped for the best. In the manner of all first-jump parachutists he hit the ground before he thought he would, landing heavily and awkwardly, the force almost winding him whilst his wounded leg gave him plain hell. The silken canopy of his parachute wreathed and billowed down directly on top of him. As soon as he could pull himself together he had to go through the blind and infuriating business of bunching and pulling until the parachute-edge came into his hands and he could lift it and see all around. He found that he had had a second escape from death. For he had landed in one of the few clear spaces amongst a mass of lava boulders, and a fall across any one of them would more than probably have broken his back.

Now he glimpsed again the house he had seen from the air. But it was dead silent and still in the sunshine, with no hint of human occupants. So still was everything that he wondered for a moment whether his sight of that group of men and women had merely been an illusion of his overstrained mind. He tried to get up on his feet but found it impossible. When he turned up a trouser leg he found a gaping hole clean through the calf of his left leg and also a smaller hole which had already swollen and was looking angry and livid. With a sigh he took stock of his other wounds, gingerly passing his hands over his head. To his relief he found that they seemed to be more painful than serious. The urgent necessity, therefore, was to get his array of holes and abrasions cleaned and dressed as soon as possible before blood poisoning set in.

Slowly and painfully, he started crawling towards the house. The front door was open but no one appeared. He realized that since they were simple peasants of the Italian countryside, they would be hiding from him, waiting to see what he would do. There was also the possibility that once they realized that he was helpless they might take a shot at him, probably with a farmer's gun, just to curry favour with the German troops who were in occupation.

The problem was a stiff one, but he decided that the danger from poison or gangrene was just as much a threat to his life as that of any armed cottager. Therefore he crawled onwards, heaved himself up against a rock and presented himself in full view of the cottage door. For a while nothing happened. Then he saw a woman looking furtively out of one of the windows. He heard whispering, and finally an aged man appeared within the shadow of the front door and called out something in Italian which he didn't understand.

Sexton gestured with his hands and patted himself to indicate that he was unarmed. He pointed to his wounds. The old man came forward cautiously, but after a careful look appeared to be satisfied and turned to call something over his shoulder. The whole family then came out of the cottage, including the usual troop of children, and he was helped inside, realizing thankfully enough that they were going to be friendly and humane.

It was while the peasant family were doing their best to clean his wounds that a couple of German soldiers arrived. They looked fierce enough, one presenting a tommy-gun at his head whilst the other made sure he had no weapons. To his astonishment, they both grinned in a friendly manner, and one asked in good English if he knew how many wounds he had.

Sexton said with grim humour that he wouldn't like to swear on oath to any exact number, but maybe the Germans would like to check up for themselves, a remark which the man translated, raising a general laugh. The Germans dropped their guns in a corner of the room and set about bathing, cleaning and bandaging him with rough skill. They told him he must be moved, and helped him outside and on to a donkey which had been brought to the door by one of the children. For a painful, dizzy hour Sexton swayed on the donkey's back with his guards beside him until he reached a large house filled with both German and Italian troops. Here he was given a bed and a plentiful, if rough, meal. But his ordeal was to come next morning, when an elderly Italian captain of the medical corps arrived to examine him. After a while, the Captain shrugged his shoulders and said something to the men around. Sexton was told to get up and was helped outside and into an olive grove, where he was lowered on to a stool.

As he did so the Italian doctor opened his surgical case, took out scissors, scalpels and other unpleasant-looking medical tools and then snapped the case shut. Having done so, he lifted Sexton's badly wounded leg and put the case beneath it, at the same time nodding to a man who stood nearby with a bottle and a cup. The man nearly filled the cup and handed it to Sexton.

"Drink," said the doctor. "Drink—quick."

Sexton took a long pull at the cup and coughed violently, for it was good, raw liquor. At the same time he began to realize why he had been brought out of the house into the olive grove. His leg wounds, now that he got a really close look at them, had a threatening appearance. He suddenly had the deadly fear that the doctor was going to amputate. That would be the reason for the hard liquor, since it was well known that the Italian forces were hopelessly short of anæsthetics. The only humane thing they could do was to get a patient drunk.

He emptied the cup, which was at once refilled and handed back to him.

"Are you going to take my leg off?" he asked, but it seemed the doctor understood little English. He merely gestured again and said "Drink", which was probably one of the few words he knew. Sexton emptied the second cup of liquor with a not-too-steady hand. The raw spirit was already beginning to work. He felt warmed and dizzy. He began to reason that whereas gangrene would almost certainly kill him within a short time, he might possibly survive a leg amputation without anæsthetic. Therefore he had better steel himself to the ordeal. While he was thinking along these lines, half a dozen pairs of hands caught hold of him, he was rigidly held . . . and the doctor started work.

It was not until long afterwards that he discovered that amputation had not been the order of the day. The doctor certainly went to work with his knife and scalpel. In a hideous nightmare of pain Sexton blacked out for a while. How long it was he doesn't know, but when he came to, he was still being held down and actually saw the doctor removing a large and jagged piece of steel from inside his leg. Then he soaked a rag in raw kerosene, pushed it into the wound with a probe, and pulled it clean through.

With the shortage of both antiseptics and anæsthetics he knew that the doctor was doing his best in the circumstances. But when it was all over he was in such a daze of pain and drunkenness that he never knew whether he had been yelling or not.

Sexton was moved from hospital to hospital after that, finally being evacuated from Sicily to the mainland. On the whole he was treated well, his wounds healed, and he began to be able to walk, although with difficulty because his leg was still in plaster. Then came the wonderful news that the Allies had landed in Anzio.

There was naturally a high jubilation amongst the wounded prisoners when this was openly admitted over the enemy wireless. Yet their joy was short-lived, for they were moved almost immediately afterwards and their Italian guards told them that the Germans had ordered all British and American prisoners-of-war to be transported to the Fatherland. All of them had heard grisly stories of concentration camps and the tortures, and Sexton for one determined that he would much prefer death to entering Germany as a prisoner.

On a crowded hospital train going north, some weeks later, he waited for his chance when the overworked guard's attention was elsewhere—and he jumped for it. By a miracle he neither killed himself nor broke his damaged leg. From that time until just before Easter 1944 he tramped the countryside, keeping well away from any Germans and living on the goodwill of the Italians, who, almost without exception, were friendly.

At first he made his way south, with the idea of trying to slip through to the American Forces holding the Anzio beach-head. But this he found to be impossible owing to the concentration of German troops round the land-side perimeter. His next idea was to get to Rome, since it was obvious that that was the great prize of any invading army. And he reasoned that it would be as good a place as any to be in when the invading troops finally arrived. The Germans had agreed not to shell and burn Paris when it was surrendered by the French. It was possible, therefore, that the Germans might not smash up the architectural gem that was Rome before they left. And he was certain there would be no attack upon it by the Allies. If he could get there and lie low it seemed to offer the best chance of survival.

When finally he reached a point 16 miles from Rome, however, his privations had so weakened him, and his wounded leg was again giving him such pain, that he dropped down by the roadside feeling that he had neither strength nor courage to go any further. How many hundreds of miles he had walked in those months he had no idea. He had lived like a beggar, and the last pair of shoes he had managed to beg from a good-natured farmer were worn through into holes.

As he sat there, a boy arrived on a bicycle and sat down to rest, giving him a nod as he did so. He had found most of the young Italians friendly, so he asked the lad if there was a German road-block ahead and what was the best way of getting round it. The boy grinned at the halting, heavily-accented Italian Sexton had managed to pick up.

"You'll never get through," he said; "you are an Americano. There is a big road-block which all must pass before getting into the city, and there they check all identification cards."

Sexton felt that the end had come. How he could get over such an obstacle he could not think. Depression settled down upon him like a cloud, and evidently he showed it.

"Why don't you take a tram?" asked the boy, laughing.

At first Sexton thought that it was a cruel, youthful joke, but as the boy went on talking he began listening with interest. There was a tramway running from the next village, not far away, right into the centre of Rome, he learned. The Germans were not in the habit of checking passengers on the trams, or if they did so, it was not a regular thing. They were mostly concerned with traffic on the highway.

Sexton had a few lire he had been hoarding with miserly care against just such an emergency. On the face of it the whole thing seemed to be crack-brained. For a man to tramp miles upon miles through the heat of valleys and the cold of mountain roads, and to finish up taking a tram to the one place he had been trying to get at all the time! Yet the more he thought of it, however crazy it was, the more he liked it.

"If I give you the money will you buy my ticket for me?" he asked. "I speak so badly. You are right. Everyone will know I am an Americano."

The boy got up and moved his bicycle out of sight behind a hedge, pulling up grass and throwing it over the frame.

"I have enough money," he said. "Enough for two fares. I'll come back and fetch my bicycle later. Now you come with me."

Sexton hobbled with his new-found young friend to the village tram-stop. When a car rumbled up beside them they boarded it and the lad paid the two fares. Then the car started off again and, as Sexton sat swaying and looking out at the sunlit countryside through the windows, he had difficulty in not laughing outright. The whole thing seemed so homely, so normal, so altogether divorced from any idea of war. Meanwhile, the miles were clicking and rumbling by at a spanking pace, all of 15 miles an hour, a speed which seemed to the utterly exhausted American pilot faster than anything his own B25 had ever managed.

He had one nasty moment to come, however. Just on the outskirts of Rome the tram slowed and then suddenly ground to a standstill. Sexton craned his neck to look past the passengers and see what was happening. To his horror he saw an armed German guard at both entrances, fore and aft of the vehicle. The guards climbed up and began moving along the centre aisle from each end, looking carefully down at the passengers.

Sexton at first imagined that they were going to ask for identification cards. This, of course, meant the end for him after all his long months of tramping and avoiding interrogation at every turn. He decided that if it came to the point he'd end the whole thing then and there. He would try to grab one of the men's rifles and make sure of taking one German with him before the second guard inevitably blasted him out of this world. He tensed himself as the man nearest him came along the aisle.

But then his heart turned over in almost-unbelieving relief. The soldiers were asking the passengers for nothing. They were merely examining baskets, turning over bundles, and probing into anything that the peasants were carrying. When the German came to Sexton, he merely glanced at the jacket he had slung across his knees and passed on without a word.

A moment or two later both the soldiers had dropped off and the tram was clanking along once more. Looking back at it, there is one American pilot who admits that he nearly fell flat in a faint out of pure relief.

Once inside the city his young friend whispered to him when the time came for them to get down at a stop. Then he led Sexton through the streets to a very comfortable apartment house where he was introduced to the boy's parents who, in spite of his wild unshaven appearance, welcomed him and took him in.

After a dead dreamless sleep in a real bed that night, Sexton luxuriated in a bath next morning, shaved off his wild beard and thankfully accepted the gift of a well-worn suit and a pair of shoes. After a good breakfast he asked what his chances were of going to earth in some part of the city.

"You must go to the Vatican," said his elder friend with a gesture.

Sexton nodded politely, although he had an instinct to chuckle. He was not a Roman Catholic by religion, but he could well understand that an act of thanksgiving to God might well be expected of him for his good fortune in having found such help. For the moment he only thought of the Vatican as the residence of the Pope and therefore, in a sense, the high church of all churches.

"Indeed, sir," he said seriously, and well he meant it, "God has been good to me, and I shall offer Him my thanks as soon as one of you good people can guide me to the Vatican. But when I have done that—which, of course, is my first duty—where do you think I may have a chance of hiding? Do you know anywhere I could get work until the city falls into the hands of my comrades?"

The man stared at him and laughed abruptly.

"Give thanks before an altar as soon as you may," he

said, "but that, my friend, was not what I meant. I was saying that you must get into the Vatican, which is a city within itself—a city within the city of Rome—and even the Germans hold it to be a sanctuary under God into which no man may set foot except at the word of His Holiness the Pope. Once a man is in there, no soldier of any nation will enter to take him away. And I can tell you that now, within the Vatican walls, there are men of all nations you can think of; Germans, Italians, English, Americans, probably even Japanese."

Light suddenly broke upon Sexton's mind. He remembered now what he had always vaguely known, that the Vatican City was neutral ground, a religious State in itself to which the countries of the world appointed their ambassadors.

"I see your point," he said slowly. "I've just never thought about it before. But—but—I wasn't brought up Roman Catholic and I guess I'd hate to pretend, just to save my skin. Moreover, it can't be easy, getting in there. I mean the Germans can't be letting anyone run through the Vatican door just when he likes."

"Your religion or beliefs make no difference whatever," said his friend. "In the Vatican there is sanctuary for all who ask it, so long as they have no ulterior motive and tell all the truth about themselves. Still, you are right about the Germans. There are SS men constantly on the watch. If they can snatch you when your foot is but a metre from the gateway they will do so. But once you are across the threshold you are safe."

For a long time Sexton, the boy and his father discussed the idea. They sketched him an outline of the Vatican City with its towering walls. They showed him the position of the gates where the Swiss guards were always on duty in their medieval striped uniforms and helmets. Here lay the real difficulty. The German SS men were always on the watch. If Sexton asked any of the Swiss guards for permission to enter, he would be questioned and there would be a delay before he was passed on to an officer. They would not let him just walk straight through. While he was talking, the SS men would undoubtedly swoop and drag him away for their own special methods of questioning before he had a chance of putting a foot within the bounds of sanctuary.

However, the boy's father had held a position with the Government before the Occupation and he knew one of the men who worked in the Vatican radio station. He telephoned this man, and asked him to be at the main gate, just to the left of the cathedral of St Peter, at a certain time that morning.

"So far, so good," he said, when he had finished his telephone conversation. "Now sit down and write a note to your American Ambassador in the Vatican City. I will give the note to my friend when he appears at the gate."

The plan was carried out and the three men went down to the magnificent square of St Peter, pausing there to look at the columns and statuary and the circling pigeons, and trying to appear as much like tourists as possible. Suddenly the father said a brief word and left them. He walked nonchalantly over to the Vatican gate and could be seen talking with someone who stood between the Swiss guards. After a while he turned and came back.

"Walk beside me, but go on looking like a tourist," he whispered. "Your note will be delivered to the secretary of your Ambassador immediately. Now talk of other things; there are two SS men, whom I have recognized, nearby. They have looked at us more than once already."

"How shall I know when I can try to get in?" breathed Sexton, who admits that at that moment a colony of butterflies seemed to have taken up residence in his stomach.

"Very soon now," said his companion. "A priest whom I shall point out to you will walk out of the gate in a moment or two. You will follow him. He will lead you for about a mile along the wall to another gate. Keep about 50 yards behind him and try not to show that you are following him. But when he goes through the second gate, you go straight through after him. Don't hesitate. Just go straight in. God be with you."

Sexton suddenly felt as though he were a little drunk and uncertain on his feet. He felt as though the eyes of the whole of Rome were upon him. He dared not look round for the SS men, but had a horrible idea that he could hear their footsteps following his own. The sunshine seemed unnaturally bright, and although he paused from time to time with his companions and admired columns and statuary, he had not the faintest remembrance of what he had seen.

"Now!" whispered his friend suddenly. "There is Monsignor. Do what I say, but don't follow too close. Shake hands with us now, and laugh and act naturally as you leave us."

How Sexton got through that little piece of play-acting he never knew. He marked the black-coated priest who had left the Vatican gates and had passed them without so much as a glance. Then, at a respectable distance, he followed the small, rather tubby figure in its flowing robe. The priest, in common with many short men, walked swiftly with short, rapid steps. Sexton's damaged leg began hurting him like the devil as he strove to walk at the same pace and yet try not to give the impression that he was following. That mile round the towering wall outside the Vatican City was the longest he ever walked in his life. At last he saw two Swiss guards in their brilliant uniforms at a gateway. They were marching a set beat in either direction, but turned and came back on either side of the gate as the priest approached. They saluted as he passed between them, standing to attention and staring rigidly at each other as Sexton hobbled towards them.

By now he was sweating profusely and his heart was in

his mouth. He could hear footsteps behind him and had a ghastly conviction that the SS men were playing cat and mouse with him. As he approached the guards, he wondered if they were going to bar his way with their pikes. It didn't seem possible that they would let him through without inquiry.

But they did. As he held on to his courage and turned to pass between them straight into the gateway, each of the guards turned outwards smartly. Each then marched off along his respective beat, taking not the slightest notice of the newcomer. It was quite evident to Sexton that the priest must have whispered something to them as he went through.

Next moment Sexton limped into Vatican City, hearing the following footsteps pass him and go straight upon their way. He was so overwrought with elation that he never saw who had been following him and now he didn't care. Then he found himself facing a smiling little man who stood beside the priest. Both of them shook hands with him.

"I am the secretary to the British Embassy," said the priest's companion. "And this is Monsignor McGough. We are informed that you are an American. Now come along and let us see whatever papers you may have."

Sexton couldn't speak for the moment, but he was thanking his lucky stars that in all his wanderings he had managed to hang on to an American identity card, which he now brought shakily out of his pocket.

. . . . .

Sexton found sanctuary in Vatican City just before Easter 1944. On the following June 5th the Americans took Rome, which the retreating Germans at least had the decency not to defend or to damage in any way. As American aircraft flew overhead and American tanks rumbled through the streets, the polyglot inhabitants of the Vatican City rushed out to welcome them. Meanwhile the Italians were throwing flowers in the path of the marching columns of troops, most of whom soon had roses sticking out of the end of their rifles and planted into their helmets.

Sexton, having reported to the first unit commander he could find, was carefully interrogated and then flown down to Foggia, the temporary headquarters of the United States 12th Air Force. There, from the Intelligence Section, he got no news of the rest of his crew except what he already knew himself, that all save one had baled out of the burning aircraft. Regretfully he gave the report that one, his co-pilot, had been killed outright when the aircraft was first hit.

From that point he was flown to Algiers, since he was rated as not medically fit to continue flying duty in action, and was officially posted home to America. On this section of his long flight home the pilot obligingly swung over the coast of Sicily and came fairly low to pass near Mount Etna. Sexton looked down at the actual spot where his B25 had crashed almost a year previously.

From Algiers he was flown to Casablanca, and he took pride in the efficiency of his own service because at 3.30 am on the following morning he was awakened and hustled off into a big C54, which immediately took off for the flight across the Atlantic via the Azores.

At last came the truly wonderful moment at about 9 pm one evening when the aircraft was swinging in over New York harbour. Sexton's eyes were a bit misty as he saw the city's lights. But before the aircraft landed and he felt the heavenly firmness of American ground beneath his feet, he had one experience which he counts as vivid as any in his whole service in the war.

In the aircraft was an important German prisoner who was being taken to America for special interrogation. Although important, he was still in his early thirties. At the sight of the lights of New York, even in their state of 'semi-black-out', he spoke instinctively.

"You Americans must be mad," he said. "Look at all that light showing. What a target your city makes for our bombers." There was an incredulous burst of laughter from the Americans around him.

"Bombers?" inquired one of them. "What bombers?"

The German stared at him and then stared down at the great city below. He started to speak but checked himself. Then he frowned deeply.

For a moment Sexton felt half-sorry for him. It was perfectly plain to see what was going on in the young German's mind. For the very first time in his life he was beginning to realize that the whole of the Nazi teaching was based on lies and braggartry. He was learning at first-hand the real truth about tales he had heard of super-long-range Nazi bombers which were supposed to have battered New York. Here was New York in all its glory, with its towering skyscrapers, its lines of piers and wharfs; and not one skyscraper-tower showing the slightest sign of damage.

The young German dragged his eyes away from the scene, so beautiful to every other man in the aircraft. From that moment onwards he sat erect, staring directly in front of him and saying not a word.

18

LAST MAN OUT

THOSE who set store by numbers may think that seven was lucky for Sergeant Reginald L. Luce. Anyway, it was dominant in his flying record. He was born on December 17th, 1915. His number in the organization, in which he learned to fly before the war, was 1777. He did most of his war flying with 77 Squadron at Topcliffe in Yorkshire (service number 911370). And on the seventh night of the seventh month in 1941 he was on his twenty-seventh operational flight as wireless operator-air gunner when the events here recorded took place. (Incidentally this peculiar record was broken by the fact that he was married on December 26th, 1946; but, as everybody knows, where a woman is involved anything can happen.)

During that summer Bomber Command had been hammering at German railway communications, with especial attention to 'Happy Valley', the aircrew name for the vast industrial district of the Ruhr which roughly corresponds to our own Black Country. This caused considerable resentment on the part of the Germans, who at that time had a most beautiful and complex plan for the conquest of Russia as well as Europe. It was extremely difficult for any Teutonic mind to grasp just why the RAF with their virtually small numbers should be so stubborn and aggressive and altogether annoying when the Herrenvolk were busy trying to subjugate the Soviets. The German High Command therefore moved all the searchlights and anti-aircraft cannon they could spare into Happy Valley and the gunners worked with vim. They made the valley a very difficult place to get into, and an equally difficult place to get out of, for all British aircraft. Nevertheless, Sergeant Luce and his comrades of Bomber Command simply wouldn't take the hint, and went on distracting German attention from the Russian front no matter how many of their friends were shot down beside them in the process.

We who are alive and in comfortable jobs today owe much of our good fortune to the slightly primitive sense of humour of those young men who just couldn't be brought to take Hitler seriously, even though they knew that they would probably get killed in opposing him.

Sergeant Luce and his comrades so typically held this point of view that they named their track out to the Ruhr Valley 'the 25a bus route'. In the Whitley aircraft in which they took off from Topcliffe aerodrome on the night of which I have to tell, there were three besides Luce who were seasoned warriors, all averaging around thirty operational flights. These were Flight Lieutenant Petley, AFC, the captain, and Sergeants G. Lightley and F. Christopher, the second-pilot and the navigator. Sergeant Wilson, the rear-gunner, was a first tripper but he was a lad they already liked well, and they all felt that he was going to shake down and give a good account of himself in his responsible, if unenviable and draughty, position.

The moon was bright in a clear summer sky as they droned away across the sleeping Yorkshire countryside and out over the sea.

Meanwhile, the bright moonlight promised that they would receive a most lively welcome from the flak gunners. There was also every chance that they might be spotted by an advance reception committee of German fighter-aircraft, more than probably Me109s, which they already knew to be stationed at Leuwarden.

As the Dutch coast passed beneath the machine, making a dull fringe to the beaten-silver expanse of the sea, Sergeant Luce got busy with his box of electrical tricks and sent his routine signal, 'crossing enemy coast'. In his small cabin he could see and hear nothing of what went forward in the rest of the world outside. Everything seemed normal enough, however, except the wireless set itself. As he worked, it went dead. He fiddled with it, made an adjustment, but was not altogether certain that it was functioning properly.

However, since he didn't care to bother his skipper with details, he leant out of his cabin to call Petley's attention and give him the thumbs-up sign that the signal had been sent. Then he had a most unpleasant surprise, for the pilot's seat was empty, and for a moment it appeared that he was entirely alone in the aircraft. He saw a vague figure standing over the forward escape hatch, wearing a parachute and beckoning him urgently. The figure crouched down, slid over the hatch-edge and disappeared.

Naturally enough Luce realized that his bother with the wireless set had meant real trouble. He knew that an order to bale out must have been given by the skipper, but owing to general circuit failure he hadn't been able to hear it over the intercom. What had caused everybody to grab their parachutes and jump he hadn't the faintest idea. In the freakish way that things have of happening to aircraft, he had felt no shock, sensed no unusual movement, and heard no alteration in the note of the engines.

As the only man left aboard, he reasoned that it was no time to debate possibilities. The obvious thing was to grab his parachute and follow the others. Accordingly, he knelt down, whipped his parachute pack from beneath his seat and clipped it on. He jerked open the mid-fuselage hatch—and had all his questions answered. Outside the hatch a roaring mass of flame was blasting back from the wing tanks in the slip-stream of the machine. There and then it was perfectly obvious that an enemy fighter must have crept up on their blind spot and exploded the tanks with a burst of cannon shells.

Luce decided to waste no further time. He was about to crawl along the gangway towards the escape hatch when he felt a sharp stabbing pain in his body, and, as far as he knows, recovered his senses a few seconds later to find himself lying flat on his face on the cabin floor.

As a matter of record, the reason for this was the enemy fighter which had come back to administer a second burst as a *coup de grâce* after having set the aircraft on fire in a first attack. A cannon shell from that second burst struck Luce in his left hip, went clean through him, chipping his spinal column on the way, and then went out again, leaving a sizeable split in his back. He lay on the floor for a while, trying fiercely to get the rights of everything whilst his senses slowly returned to him. Once he could think connectedly the all-important fact came back into his mind : he must get out of the aircraft, and quickly, before the blazing tanks finally blew up.

Luce got weaving as best he could. As he dragged himself forward towards the pilot's seat, his left side was completely paralysed and he had no feeling in either his left arm or leg. Even so he got to the back of the seat, clawed himself up, and half-blindly caught hold of the control stick in the process. Naturally enough, in doing so he wrenched it back but, as he realized later, one of the aileron wires must have been shot through, for the stick movement immediately put the damaged and blazing Whitley into a barrel-roll.

What happened in the course of that roll he could never clearly remember afterwards. All he knows is that the aircraft somehow righted itself and there came a moment in which he realized that it was roughly on a level keel while he himself was draped helplessly over the pilot's seat. Since his tiny nightmare world had reached some kind of equilibrium he put out one more violent effort. He dragged himself out of the machine and reached to grab at the radio mast. By that time vague waves were weaving within his mind. He knew it was crazy to jump from above the aircraft and, anyway, the effort was beyond him. With his last will-power he lurchingly forced himself to stand up on his good leg. At the same time he took a blind chance and pulled at the ripcord of his parachute.

In the next second he was aware of passing the tailplane of the aircraft at appalling speed, missing it by what seemed like inches. His parachute, of course, had inflated and whipped him off the doomed machine. After that he didn't remember anything more until consciousness came back to him while he was hanging in his harness and drifting down the silent moonless sky over the flat countryside of Holland.

Luce was badly wounded, and he knew it. For the time being he was mainly thankful that he had somehow managed to get himself out of a spectacular blazing coffin which had been gyrating round the sky. Then as he hung in his harness there was a thudding explosion from below which actually swayed him beneath his parachute. As he glanced down he saw a sudden uprush of bursting flame and sparks which marked where the Whitley had made its last landing.

Very shortly afterwards Luce made his own landing in the forest of Leuwarden at, as far as he can judge, 2.30 am on July 8th. It was easy because his parachute caught in the trees. After a few jerks and a spectacular crackling and breaking of branches he finally came to rest, still in his harness, swaying in the darkness. Since he had no means of knowing how high he was from the ground, he very sensibly decided not to use his release gear and drop clear until dawn broke.

From then until around 6 am, when there was light enough for him to see his surroundings, was by no means a pleasant period. A parachute harness is not the most comfortable place of repose for a seriously wounded man. However, when at last he could make out where the ground was, he found it less than 3 feet below his dangling boots. He knocked his release gear undone, dropped down in a heap, and took what pleasure he could from being actually upon hard, dry land.

In one way his peculiar luck—if you like to regard it as such—had worked to advantage. It proved afterwards that his long period of hanging in the harness may have saved his life. The harness suit had compressed his wounds with the result that the blood had coagulated. Meanwhile, he had a few cigarettes in his flying-suit, a chocolate bar and some spearmint gum, which kept him going. Still, that was not an over-generous ration for two whole days.

From the time he baled out, Luce spent almost

precisely that time in the Leuwarden forest before he was found. Throughout the long, hot summer day of July 8th he lay helplessly on the ground beneath the trees. From time to time he heard a circular saw working somewhere in the forest. Whenever it stopped he got together what strength he had left and yelled and shouted. But no one came. The saw worked on and on, its thin harsh note like the monotonous cry of some nightmare bird throughout the long hours of the afternoon. Then it stopped and in deep silence the gathering twilight gradually gave place to night.

Luce got through that second night in comparative comfort. It is more than probable that he was unconscious for long periods without realizing it. He lay where he was until the sun woke him again. At roughly 9 am he heard something moving in the bracken. He saw three Dutch foresters, who had either seen the remains of his parachute festooned in the tree or had just stumbled upon him. There they were standing over him and staring in obvious amazement.

Luce knew a little French and German, but no Dutch at all. At first there was gabble and pantomime. By signs they asked if he could walk. When he showed his helplessness they knelt down and made fumbling attempts to tie branches to his legs as splints. Then he made them realize that the trouble was in his back, and when they saw the obvious signs of it, the three took counsel together in shocked whispers. He understood them to say they must "get the Bosche". What that meant, Luce had a slight idea, although he didn't like the sound of it.

Two of the men went off, but once they had gone the third drew a large knife and came down to kneel beside him with a somewhat alarming smile. The moment was not pleasant. Luce had plenty of fighting spirit left in him but no strength. However, he almost chuckled in thankfulness when the Dutchman started cutting the RAF brass buttons off his uniform. As he did so he grinned, announced "RAF buttons, goot . . ." and, having cut off the lot, fell to polishing them upon the sleeve of his coat.

The other foresters were as good as their word. In about half an hour a German captain arrived and, jerking his pistol from its holster, asked Luce to give up his weapons. When it was obvious that the helpless prisoner had none, the German dropped his military ferocity, became human and gave him a cigarette.

"Soon you will be looked after," he said. "Dere shall be no more worry. For you, *mein freund*, dees war is ofer."

Less than an hour later Luce was in the Leuwarden Convent Hospital, where all his personal possessions were taken from him and he never saw them again. However, he received good and immediate medical attention and some days later was moved to a hospital in Amsterdam, where he was tucked up in one of a ward of fifty empty beds, which he found to be somewhat lonely and depressing. But there were two Dutch women cleaners who crept into the room very early each morning, knelt by his bed and kissed both his hands.

From that point he was moved to thirteen different prison camps and hospitals in Holland and Germany and is ready to admit that he has to thank a German doctor, Professor Schmiedem, for saving his life with a delicate operation. Although the Professor was seventy-seven years old, he practically rebuilt Luce's bowel passage which the cannon shell had torn apart. The doctor also enabled him to go on living without the top left-hand side of his pelvic girdle. With this help and the constant attention of two brother prisoners, Major Lorst and Major Martin, both of whom had been captured at Dunkirk, he gradually won back to a normal physical life.

During this time he became known to the Germans and their staff doctors as the *Wundermensch*—or wonder boy—for his fantastic powers of survival. Finally, he was repatriated in 1943 and demobilized in 1944 with the rank of Warrant Officer. In August of that year he was fortunate in choosing the right day upon which to visit the Roebuck Hotel at Buckhurst Hill in Essex. There he met Cecilia, the girl to whom he is now happily married.

Mr Luce is today a local government officer in Dagenham. He leads a full life and can enjoy an hour of swimming and drive his own car. A recent letter from him lies before me, and it is typical of so many I received in preparing this record.

He asks, "Please just keep to facts and, if you publish it, dedicate it to the memory of the other chaps who were with me in the aircraft, all of whom died and now lie together in the small Dutch village of Osterbeck'.

Luce thinks that, in the hurry to abandon aircraft at the time of the fire outbreak, his comrades must have jumped facing the nose instead of the tail. This would almost inevitably mean that they must have been struck by the machine, which again seems likely since the good Dutch folk who found them and gave them a Christian burial reported that none of them bore wounds.

19

GOING OUT AT 500—PLUS

When, as a lad of eighteen, I made my first flight and took my first lesson in the business of piloting, I was considerably disappointed. At that age an indulgent mamma had already made me the present of a motor-cycle, the design and balance of which I forthwith ruined by drilling out the piston-skirt and connecting-rod and by adding stronger valve springs (as I later discovered, too strong for the valves themselves). However, in the periods when it *would* run I could get a top speed of 65 miles an hour out of it, and naturally felt highly pleased with myself.

It will be understood, therefore, that when I sat behind my first flying-instructor and saw the airspeed indicator showing only 45 miles an hour when the machine lifted into the air, I felt that this business of flying was not going to be half as thrilling as I had expected. I was destined to learn very differently in a short space of time, but that is neither here nor there.

To come to the point, that first aircraft, an Avro 504 with a 50-horse-power Gnome rotary engine, was just about as fast as my motor-cycle when flying level on full throttle, in spite of which it had been a fully operational, fighting aircraft in combat only a few years beforehand. Incidentally, in basic form, it remained the standard trainer for the Royal Air Force for years afterwards.

In the thirty-odd years since that day speeds of service fighters have, as everyone knows, increased some eleven times over. The international competition for more and more speed has raised enormous problems for engine and airframe designers. One of the greatest problems, however, concerned the parachute. In short, it became clear that no airman would, without assistance, be able to get out of an aircraft moving at 500 miles an hour and open the normal-type parachute. The reasons are fairly simple. Even if a man did manage to get out into a 500-mile-an-hour blast, he would more than probably be smashed against the tail. If that didn't happen the blast would knock him unconscious, if it didn't kill him outright, and he would certainly be unable to pull his release-ring. Again, even if by a miracle he did so, the parachute would be burst as soon as it inflated.

The answer to this was found in the ejector-seat, which is now, in different forms, a standard fitting in all high-speed jet aircraft. The principle of this is simple in outline, but highly complicated in actual fact. Briefly, the pilot's seat as a whole is made detachable from the airframe. When it is necessary to bale out the pilot pulls a release which automatically throws off the canopy above his head. Then he reaches up and pulls a 'blind' which comes directly down in front of his face. This also automatically releases his seat and fires an explosive cartridge beneath it.

Thus the seat with the pilot sitting in it is blown clean out of the machine. The blind over the pilot's face saves him from the worst effect of the 500-mile-an-hour blast. The solid seat in which he is still sitting helps his body to take the shock and saves him from breaking bones, especially by contact with any part of the machine as he goes out. One of the greatest advantages of the ejector-seat is, of course, that it carries the pilot well clear of the tail-plane, fin and rudder.

It will be understood that the pilot is held firmly to the seat by his safety harness, which is attached to the seat and not the airframe. Directly both seat and pilot are ejected a drogue is automatically released to slow their progress as they plummet down the sky. At this point the pilot releases his safety harness, drops clear of the seat, and then pulls the release of his personal parachute.

Low-level ejections at high speed, governed by an automatic system (which will be mentioned later), have been so successful that men have 'come out' as low as 200 feet and survived, while successful ejections of dummies right down to 50 feet have been accomplished.

So far so good, but the problem did not end there. From the earliest days of the first war, 'fighting altitude' for both bombers and pursuit aircraft has steadily been getting higher and higher; for many years pilots have been provided with oxygen. Now, with 'fighting altitude' reaching up to 40000 feet and more, there is another danger which threatens any man who has to bale out.

At that height an airman cannot expect to remain conscious without a supply of oxygen for more than about five seconds.

On most ejector-seats there is an emergency oxygen-supply which will automatically keep the pilot supplied for about ten minutes after he has left the machine. Even so, there was a great danger to be foreseen in leaving the final opening of a man's parachute to his own action, when he had slowed down sufficiently, or reached a safe altitude.

There was an all-important point which still had to be considered. Quite apart from the lack of oxygen, the pilot might be seriously wounded, and unconscious for that reason alone. So once more designers provided a solution. In addition to the automatic drogues which were released from the falling seat to slow its speed, the designers added different forms of final automatic opening of the pilot's *own* parachute. One of these is worked by a barometer-mechanism which will release the pilot's seat-harness, usually between 5000 and 10000 feet. Since the seat falls tilted, with the pilot facing downwards, this naturally means that, at that height, he will leave the seat and fall free. A static line then pulls out his own personal parachute and ensures that it will open—whether or not he is conscious. This is also achieved in some designs by a mechanical action governed by a time-mechanism.

For final safety in any design there is an 'over-riding control' by which a pilot can actuate the whole series of movements himself.

Well, there is the principle of the whole thing. For the unscientific minded, I will just say that a barometer is not only an apparatus for telling you when a depression is approaching from Iceland; it is also a 'thing' which will accurately measure height, since air pressure and height come to the same thing in this sense.

There is only one more small point for me to add before I go ahead and tell the story of a Flight Lieutenant who asks me to give his name only as 'Johnny' and Flying Officer J. R. Rumbelow, both of the Royal Air Force, who, only a few months ago, collided in their high-speed Sabre jet aircraft, fired themselves out in their ejector-seats and, I am happy to say, survived to tell me their stories.

Since the Sabre is basically an American design it is equipped with an American ejector-seat which differs in very small ways from those I have just described. It is not fully automatic and has no face-blind. This does not matter, because pilots these days wear special crash helmets ('bone-domes') and visors in place of the older-fashioned sun-glasses. This equipment gives their faces full protection from the forward blast of ejection.

Apart from this, the Sabre seat is actuated by three levers. The right-hand lever blows the aircraft canopy off with the assistance of explosive rivets. A lever on the left hand is then pulled up to tighten and lock the pilot's harness which holds him to the seat. Final action is to jerk up a second lever on the right-hand side which can only function after the first one has been pulled. This explodes the seat out clear of the aircraft and brings the slowing-down drogues into action.

It may sound complicated, but it is simple enough in action. There are only three levers to pull. All R/T leads, oxygen-connections and such gear are automatically broken in the act of ejection. The emergency ten-minute oxygen-supply housed in the ejected seat also starts to work by automatic means.

But in this type of seat the pilot still has to judge his time and pull the release to free himself from the seat and open his personal parachute.

Rumbelow and Johnny are members of a famous Royal Air Force fighter squadron which is now stationed in the North of England. They fly Sabre 4s—Canadian-built single-seater day-fighters, equipped with J47-GE-13 turbo-jet engines made by the General Electric Company. These aircraft with their sharply swept back wings were developed from the American F86 Sabre, which has a top speed of over 670 mph, a Service ceiling—the top height which they can normally reach—of around 50000 feet and, when fully loaded, weigh in the region of 16500 lb. It was an American Sabre incidentally which formerly held the world air speed record of 715.697 mph. In addition they have a high initial rate of climb, although this drops off with altitude.

In the normal course of peacetime duty, on a clear day of last summer, Johnny was detailed as the leader of a section of four aircraft, in a formation of eight, to carry out battle-formation exercises at high altitude. Additionally, two 'bouncing' aircraft of the same type were detailed to attack the formation during flight. In this sense the words 'bouncing' and 'attack' are Air Force language for the same thing.

Johnny, leading his section, had Flying Officer Rumbelow as his number two. Directly the aircraft had whistled off the runway they climbed straight up to a height of 28000 feet. There, in perfectly clear weather, Johnny watched carefully for the mock attack he knew would be coming.

Suddenly he caught sight of the 'bouncing' Sabre which began its attack from the rear of the formation and slightly to the port (left) side. Johnny watched the attacker coming in on a line from port to starboard, and judged its distance carefully until it went out of sight astern of him at about 800 yards. At this point he snapped the appropriate order through his microphone to his section: "Break, port—go". At the same time he turned his own aircraft through about 30–40 degrees.

Then he received an unpleasant shock. He suddenly realized that Sabre No2 of his section, piloted by Rumbelow, was converging rapidly with his own aircraft. At .7 mach (about 500 miles per hour) when aircraft are only a few feet apart, there is not a great deal of time to do much about anything. He jammed over his controls, doing his best to avoid collision, but at the same time realized that it was inevitable. A second later his port wing smashed against Rumbelow's fuselage just aft of his cockpit.

Johnny was thrown over straight away into a fast spin which soon became inverted. He recovered upright position but found he could not hold it. Still spinning, his aircraft went over on its back again. A glance at his altimeter showed him that he was below 10000 feet, and he decided it was time to get out.

He jettisoned his canopy, went through the regulation drill and, in his own words, "everything worked like a dream. My parachute opened with a jerk, but all the rest, including the landing, proved the text-book to be quite right."

As far as Rumbelow was concerned, however, things went far from normally. Directly he heard his leader's order to break he obeyed, making a sharp diving turn to port. Then his aircraft suddenly flicked over on to its back and started to spin wildly in an inverted position. He had felt no shock of collision. He had not seen anything of Johnny's aircraft as it came into him. He had no idea that anything untoward had happened until he had gone over into the inverted spin and was automatically taking recovery action.

His first idea was that he had gone into a spin out of a normal diving turn . . . for some reason which he was not, at that moment, inclined to believe was his own fault. He just thought he had tried to turn too hard at altitude, and the aircraft had flicked into a spin. The impression became very much more vivid during the next few seconds as the spin continued, no matter what he did with his controls. In his own words: "I tried every action I could think of, but the aircraft continued its mad gyrations while I could see the earth spinning crazily through the top of my canopy. It seemed very unreal and I hoped I would soon wake up to find it all nothing but a very bad dream."

Rumbelow became convinced that it was not a dream

as the Sabre started a violent pitching action while still spinning. Then he heard the voice of his leader, Johnny, through his earphones. Johnny was saying: "I'm out of control. I'm baling out."

One of the other pilots in the section initiated a 'May-day' call, which is the code word for distress to put all RAF rescue organizations into action.

This was the first indication Rumbelow had that there had been any kind of an accident at all. Naturally, since they had been in close formation, he realized that some-one had probably collided with him and damaged his aircraft. While this was going through his head he sud-denly realized that dense smoke was filling his cockpit. He guessed that his aircraft was on fire and decided it was time to bale out, too.

This was just as well since, as he afterwards discovered, the whole of his fuselage from just behind the cockpit had been smashed off. He was, in fact, going down the sky, upside-down, in a super-high-speed aircraft that was minus a tail.

As far as Rumbelow remembers in that somewhat hectic moment, he only pulled up his first right-hand lever to eject his canopy, at the same time jerking his legs back on to the foot rests and bracing himself for the tremendous air blast he knew would enter the cockpit as soon as the canopy had gone. And that, as a matter of fact, is all he does remember until he realized that he was completely clear of the aircraft, catapulting through the sky in his seat.

What actually happened neither he nor anyone else can say with certainty. It is possible that he went through the regulation three-lever 'drill'. On the other hand, it is equally possible that his seat was ejected prematurely, which may be the result of the fact that what remained of his aircraft was on fire.

In any case, he only knows that when he found himself in the open air he was heavily dazed, but managed to pull himself together and release his seat harness before yanking at his parachute rip-cord, pulling it out to the full length of his arm.

Now he knew the reason for his dazed condition. His head hurt and he realized he must have struck it against something and knocked himself silly during the process of ejection.

However, after he had pulled the rip-cord his parachute opened without any noticeable jerk. Rumbelow looked up, saw it full and billowing above him . . . and decided that it looked rather small. He had no idea of the rate at which he was falling, but even so he had a great feeling of security as he swung gently at the end of the rigging lines in a silence that was most pleasant and comforting after the general uproar and the violent motions he had been through during the previous minute or so.

He looked down and caught sight of the remains of his aircraft which was dropping fast below, blazing like a torch and still spinning madly. He stopped worrying about the size of his parachute and decided that he wasn't so badly off after all.

At that time he judged his height to be around 10000 feet. His helmet and oxygen-mask gear had gone. When he reached up to touch his face he found that it was bleeding slightly from a graze on his forehead. But now in the cool, fresh air his senses cleared and, in his own words, "Otherwise, I felt fine."

The final descent to the ground did not seem to take long and, as he got closer to the earth, he was thankful to see that he was coming down on open ground and not amongst houses, factories or railway lines. Like most other parachute first-jumpers he saw the ground coming up quickly, made a careful judgement of distance and prepared to land and roll in the regulation manner, in the middle of which he actually landed with an enormous bump which knocked all the wind out of his body.

When he could collect himself he struggled to his feet, freed himself from his gear and 'experienced a great feeling of relief to be safely on earth again'.

While he was about the business of rolling up his parachute and its shroud lines, people appeared and he learned from them that Johnny had already landed safely and was at a farm about a mile away, making his telephone report to the Squadron. Rumbelow carried his parachute to the farm.

There the two met. Johnny, after making his report, had been having a look at the still-smoking wreck of his own aircraft which lay nearby.

The conversation which followed between the two was as typical as any Air Force conversation could be:

"Hello, Johnny, I'm bloody glad to see you."

"I'm bloody glad to see you too."

"I didn't hear any call from you so I began to wonder if you'd made it."

"Oh, yes, I was OK. What height were you when you went out?"

"About 7000, or possibly a little less."

"I think I was a bit higher—10 or 15. Nothing much left of my aircraft."

"No, there wouldn't be. Mine's as flat as a pancake, too."

There was a slight pause. Johnny added that a helicopter had been sent out from base to pick them up and was on its way. Rumbelow sighed.

"Pity," he said, regretfully. "I know a girl who lives about a mile away from here, and if it wasn't for that damned helicopter we could both have gone over to her place to wait for transport."

As things were, however, nothing could be done about it. Shortly afterwards they were once again in the air in the helicopter, windmilling their dutiful way back to base. But as they went they looked out to see the remains of their aircraft which had crashed and burned out not far apart, and close to the main road between Bridlington and Driffield.

. . . . .

By way of ending this book I will merely make one small reference to the future. Rocket-type aircraft developed in America have already flown well in excess of 1000 miles an hour. It is almost inevitable that in the next few years both fighter and bomber aircraft of the Royal Air Force will be flying at these speeds. Today, as I write these lines, I have just read a report from an official American quarter which announces that at such speed it is unlikely that, even with an ejector-seat, the pilot would remain alive if he got clear of his aircraft. A friend of mine who was reading the report with me said mordantly, "That's where we came in! In our day we didn't have any parachutes at all. So the boys in future will have to take it—and like it—just as their papas did."

Personally, I don't think it will come to that. Experiments are already being made with entirely enclosed cockpits, the whole of which can be ejected from the machine so that the pilot's body is totally protected from the blast. Of course, if either the detachable cockpit or the pilot has been punctured by enemy attack there will be certain depressing complications.

But chaps who worry overmuch about things of that kind don't usually find themselves in the Air Forces of the world, anyway.

PAN Books of True War Adventure

(For a full list of PAN War books, see current edition of PAN RECORD)

Edward Lanchbery
AGAINST THE SUN

The story of Wing-Commander Roland Beamont, DSO, OBE, DFC, who has achieved fame since the War as the test pilot of Britain's supersonic prototype fighter P1, which has exceeded the speed of sound in level flight. He also tested the Canberra jet bomber and took it across the Atlantic and back in a single day. No less stirring were his adventures as a Battle of Britain pilot, train-buster, night fighter-pilot and prisoner-of-war. *Illustrated Great PAN* 2/6

George Millar, DSO, MC
HORNED PIGEON

In this new PAN volume the author describes his adventures early in the war. Taken prisoner by the Italians in North Africa, he made a vain effort to escape from Italy after the Italian surrender, but was transferred to Germany. Undaunted, he tried again—and was successful. French 'underground' workers helped him to reach Paris where he met Resistance leaders and British agents and lived in many strange households. Finally he got away over the Pyrenees to Gibraltar and home to England. Writing in the *Daily Mail*, Peter Quennell described *Horned Pigeon* as "the best and most exciting book of war experiences I have yet encountered." *PAN Giant* 3/6

George Millar, DSO, MC
MAQUIS

After his escape the author of *Horned Pigeon* became a British agent working closely with the French Resistance during the closing stages of the war. His job was to train, organise and arm the rapidly growing Maquis bands of a large area, and to select for them the sabotage targets most likely to aid the advancing Allied armies. Always on the run, he many times narrowly escaped from Gestapo cordons or outright clashes with German troops. The many colourful characters with whom he lived and fought are vividly described. *Great PAN* 2/6

PAN BOOKS LIMITED

8 HEADFORT PLACE, LONDON, S.W.1